1932–1992

THE JUBILEE YEARS

Take a close look at your *Evening Post* tonight and you'll find that the proud boast is still there for everyone to see.

'The paper all Bristol asked for and helped to create'

Sixty years ago on April 18th, 1932 when the very first edition of the new paper carrying that line appeared on the streets outside the Post's headquarters on the corner of Silver Street and Broadmead, there were crowds cheering, men flinging their hats in the air with delight and rounds of applause that could be heard strects away.

Why all this excitement? Why the fervour? Why this extraordinary relationship between a paper and its readers?

Because the Post was born a very special newspaper with a very special readership . . . and that has been its story ever since.

All Britain's major provincial cities have their own evening papers but none of them has a pedigree as proud and exciting as the Post's.

It was founded by a tightly-knit, deeply dedicated group of enthusiasts, business people, journalists, printers, advertising staff and their aides. It was funded by Bristolians who took a crusading pride in a paper of their own.

And it was a success from the day it started, at the height of Bristol's bitter press war in the late 1920s and early 1930s, and the huge newspaper empires which had carved up the city's publications—just as they had done in so many other British cities—were stunned to find an unexpected rival on their hands.

It was the brand new *Evening Post*.

Launching the paper Bristol wanted had been made possible thanks to the zeal of the founders and the rush by shareholders big and small to support the public appeal launched by the Bishop of Malmesbury, no less.

And producing the Post were ex-employees of the old *Evening Times and Mirror* which had been bought up and then closed down 12 weeks before to leave the field clear for the recently-launched *Evening World*.

Bristolians had been infuriated by the closure. They wanted their old family friend the *Times and Mirror* back and when the ex-T and M staffers came out with their paper printed on second-hand presses in a hastily-converted leather factory on Broadmead, Bristol knew their wishes had come true. The good old firm was back in business.

It wasn't plain sailing, of course. There was a war of words, a war of nerves, a war of big money newspaper competitions and a war of scoops as the Post took on the far better financed *Evening World* and beat it, blow by blow.

But this book isn't about the internal politics of the newspaper industry. It isn't about the characters who have staffed the *Post* over the six decades which followed that heady launch.

It is about how the *Evening Post* has, over the years, reflected events big and small, local and national, and captured the flavour of its circulation area, its people and the times.

There have been huge public events like the maiden flights of the beautiful Brabazon and the sleek, supersonic Concorde at Filton and the return of the s.s. *Great Britain* in one of the 20th century's most romantic rescue operations.

There have been the tragedies—the smashing of the old city in those appalling nights of the Blitz in the bitter winter of 1940/41 and the Basle air disaster of 1973, the greatest single loss of life suffered by Bristolians since World War II.

All the glamour and fun of life in a great city have been reported too, from the Hollywood chic that Bristol-born Cary Grant always brought on his visits home, to the yeah-yeah days when the Beatles brought the house down at the Colston Hall.

Royalty has come to Bristol many times. The dashing Prince of Wales was in the city in the early 1930s, encouraging the unemployed, visiting the brand new council houses in Knowle and the pretty young Princess Elizabeth came in 1950 and the crowds in Bedminster loved her.

Chilling moments too, of course. Grim murders to be reported and the doubts that crept over Bristol when the last person was hanged at Horfield prison.

The city's changing look has been chronicled, from the destruction of the wartime blitzes and sweeping clearances to make way for great new roads to the rise of the swish 1950s department stores, towering 1960s office blocks and glittering glass palaces of the 1980s.

Six days a week, 52 weeks a year for 60 years, with hardly a break, the paper's reporters and photographers have shown readers how Bristol and the world changed in the Depression of the 30s, the War Years, the post-war rebuilding era, the You've Never Had It So Good 50s, Swinging Sixties, unsure 70s and Margaret Thatcher era of the 80s. Now come the nineties and new stories to tell.

There have been many changes in the Post itself. I joined the paper about half-way through its story when we were still in that old leather factory on Broadmead.

The roof leaked—one day the news desk had to call in a supply of umbrellas to stop water pouring over that morning's batch of typed stories—and mice nested in the piles of newspapers which littered the newsroom.

Some of the older reporters still wore hats and the day always began with the early-morning smell of frying onions from the Seven Seas Chinese restaurant next door, the aroma pouring in through the fan above the crime reporter's desk.

The building was dusty, musty and noisy with the clatter of typewriters, the vibrating roar of the presses and the yells and horns as the vans whizzed in and out of Silver Street below whisking the next edition away.

The Post changed size to a big format and changed its address in the 1970s, abandoning tatty Silver Street for smart new offices in Temple Way and then changed size back again in the 1980s to everyone's relief.

The paper looks different today, of course. Colour and a snappy, Nineties

HOLD THE FRONT PAGE

60 Years of great stories from the Evening Post

James Belsey

EVENING POST

First published in 1992
by Redcliffe Press Ltd.,
49 Park Street, Bristol.

© Bristol United Press Ltd.

ISBN 1 872971 42 3

British Library Cataloguing-in-Publication Data.
A catalogue record of this book is available
from the British Library.

Published for Bristol United Press Ltd.
by Redcliffe Press, Bristol.
Typeset and printed by The Longdunn Press Ltd., Bristol.

HOLD THE FRONT PAGE

60 Years of great stories from the Evening Post

James Belsey

EVENING POST

First published in 1992
by Redcliffe Press Ltd.,
49 Park Street, Bristol.

© Bristol United Press Ltd.

ISBN 1 872971 42 3

British Library Cataloguing-in-Publication Data.
A catalogue record of this book is available
from the British Library.

Published for Bristol United Press Ltd.
by Redcliffe Press, Bristol.
Typeset and printed by The Longdunn Press Ltd., Bristol.

Press time at the old Evening Post building in Silver Street, as delivery men rush to get papers on the street.

smartness contrast sharply with the format that first appeared in 1932.

The newsroom òf April 18th, 1992 would be unrecognisable to the Post pioneers of that great day 60 years ago. They'd be astonished to see computers, colour TV sets monitoring news on the main channels and satellite stations and all the paraphernalia of a hi-tech newspaper in the late 20th century.

But if the technology has changed, the relationship between city and paper hasn't. Reporters out and about with notebooks are as familiar a sight as they were half a century ago—'I'm from the Post'.

And the relationship between paper and readers hasn't, either. It's still the click of the postbox flap, the muffled thud as the paper falls in the hall and the family's favourite read just as it was back in the early 1930s.

This is the story of the *Evening Post*—seen through 60 years of the stories that have appeared in the Post. They tell the tale of the times.

5

BRISTOL
EVENING POST

THE PAPER YOU HAVE SO EAGERLY AWAITED.

No. 1   (Regd. as a newspaper.)   **MONDAY, APRIL 18, 1932.**   ONE PENNY

SLENDER HOPES OF A POPULAR BUDGET

Times Too Uncertain for Reduction of Taxation

RIVAL CLAIMS OF
BEER AND TEA

BENEFITS, IF ANY, TO BE SHARED
EQUALLY AMONG ALL

RELIEF FOR PARENTS?

POSSIBILITY OF LOWER DUTY ON
CHEAP CINEMA SEATS

(Evening Post Political Correspondent)

TAXPAYERS are awaiting with keen anticipation to-morrow's Budget, and various sections are hoping for some alleviation of their burdens. Many hopes, it is to be feared, however, may be dashed.

The relative claims of beer and tea drinkers are expected to form an interesting part of the Chancellor's speech, and a reduction in the beer duty is generally expected.

The tariff revenue will help Mr. Chamberlain, but no considerable reduction in taxation is likely.

MINISTERS LEARN SECRETS

IN the course of a special meeting of the Cabinet at No. 10, Downing Street, this morning, Ministers heard for the first time the Budget secrets from Mr. Neville Chamberlain, the Chancellor of the Exchequer.

This was the customary meeting of the Cabinet which is always held just before the Budget—sometimes the day before and sometimes on the same morning—at which the Chancellor outlines his proposals and the main features of his speech to all the Cabinet Ministers.

BUDGET COMPLETE

In political circles, however, there is some speculation as to whether the holding of the "Budget meeting" of the Cabinet on the day before Budget Day is a sign that Mr. Chamberlain is putting forward something specially new. Another theory which has some credence is that the tariff proposals arising from the report of the Import Duties Advisory Committee are regarded by Mr. Chamberlain as necessitating some special consultation within the Cabinet.

Mr. Chamberlain, with his precious manuscript, walked through from the Treasury to No. 10, Downing Street, by the underground passage.

Prior to this meeting, apart from high officials at the Treasury, only the Prime Minister and one or two of his principal colleagues have shared the secrets.

The Budget is now complete. The finishing touches were put to it by Mr. Neville Chamberlain over the week-end at his London-house in Eaton Square.

MARKING TIME

What are the secrets carried to No. 10 to-day in the red dispatch box which has held the secrets of so many Budgets? Hopes should not be too sanguine.

Times are out of joint for Mr. Chamberlain to attempt to make his first Budget a popular one. Nothing can be really popular that does so: reduce taxation, and it is too early in an uncertain year to dare to expect this.

Disarmament, Reparations, and war debts have all to be decided internationally, while Empire policy awaits Ottawa in July.

In the absence of data which Geneva, Lausanne and Ottawa will give him, Mr. Chamberlain must be provisional and hypothetical in some of his calculations. The Budget will "mark time" in respect of awaiting international developments, and if a second Budget has to come it may be one of relief.

From the revenue point of view Mr. Chamberlain has also to consider that the £237,000,000 from Income-tax, which forms so creditable a part of the £771,000,000 of

(Continued on Page 18)

An
Explanation

IT is necessary to say, as we have no intention of misleading our readers, that the size of our opening issues has been dictated by the large spaces advertisers desired to take.

❖   ❖   ❖

AS it is we have to-day had to hold over many columns of advertisements.

❖   ❖   ❖

THE average size of the Evening Post for some time, until our equipment has been extended, may be 16 pages (with a limit placed on advertising space) if we are to meet in time the enormous circulation demand.

❖   ❖   ❖

WE feel confident the public will appreciate this and the whole of the position as it obtains, and that they will be quite content to march forward with us to the regular bigger issues directly they are possible.

(Please also see Page 6.)

Bright Periods

S.W. England and S. Wales—Moderate or light north-east or north wind, backing; mainly fair, with bright periods; rather cool; local ground frost at night. Further Outlook—Unsettled in the North; mainly fair in the South.

Lighting-up Time—8.9 p.m. to 5.16 a.m.

BRADMAN FOR CANADA

A strong team of Australian cricketers, including Don Bradman, C. V. Grimmett, W. H. Ponsford, and S. McCabe, which has the former Test player, A. A. Mailey, is bringing to Canada this summer, will play seventeen matches.

The team, which will be captained by V. Y. Richardson, of South Australia, is due to arrive in British Columbia on June 16.

REVUE FOLLIES—Queenie Ray, the charming star in "Follies of Buenos Aires," at Bristol Hippodrome.

Bristol's
New Loan
Success

LISTS CLOSED
THIS MORNING

IMMEDIATE success attended the new issue of £2,250,000 Bristol Corporation 4½ per cent. Redeemable Stock, which was issued at 100½, the lists for the cash applications being closed at 9.10 this morning.

Applications were invited for conversion of Bristol Corporation 5½ per cent. stock, 1932-42, holders of which were offered an equal amount of the new 4½ per cent. stock, in exchange for their present security which, if not converted, is to be paid off in cash on August 1 next. The new stock is repayable at par not later than May 1 1962, but the Corporation may redeem the stock at any time on or after May 1 1952, on giving three months' calendar notice.

As regards conversion applications, the list will remain open until Thursday.

In some quarters the price of 100½ per cent. was considered rather high in view of the fact that some similar loans have been made at 99½.

Bristol Corporation loans have always been eagerly sought after, and the present success is another instance of the high esteem in which Bristol's credit is held.

In the case of West Bromwich, which made a similar loan last week at 99½, dealings commenced to-day at ½ premium—equal to 99½.

BRISTOL WAR
MEMORIAL

Official Date of Unveiling
Ceremony

The Evening Post is able exclusively to announce that Bristol's War Memorial, now being prepared in Colston Avenue, will be unveiled on Sunday, June 26.

The ceremony will be performed by General Sir William Birdwood.

BANK HOLD-UP

STAFF MENACED AND OVER
£1,000 STOLEN

Over £1,000 was stolen from the till of the Commercial Bank, Denny, near Falkirk, to-day.

Two men entered the bank, and while one menaced the staff, the other stole the contents of the till. They then went off in a two-seater motor-car.

BRISTOL WILLS

Miss Mary Ordelia Swift, of 23, West Park, Redland, Bristol, at one time principal of St. Margaret's School, Bristol, who died January 19 last, left estate of the gross value of £6,827 16s. 1d., with net personalty £6,578 1s 5d. Probate has been granted to her sister, Miss Clara Amelia Swift, of the same address, the surviving executor.

She left £100 each to Edith Julion and Ethel Coleridge Tucker and all of her property to her sister, Clara Amelia Swift.

Mrs. Ann Pluniger, of 9, Beaconsfield Road, Clifton, Bristol, who died on February 1 last, aged 80 years, widow of Mr. T. Pinninger of Beckhampton, Wilts, left estate of the gross value of £3,196 3s. 3d., with net personalty £1,465 10s. 11d.

Bogus Telegram to
Missing Boy's Parents

DETECTIVES SEARCH OF BOARDING
HOUSES AND HOTELS

DESPITE an intensive search there is still no trace of Leslie Beale, the 15-year-old schoolboy, who disappeared last Wednesday morning from his parents' home at Islington after he had left to deliver a parcel to his grandmother, a short distance away.

A telegram was received by his parents the same night, ostensibly from their son, telling them not to worry.

It was stated to-day that the police are convinced that the message was not sent by the boy, and they are strongly of the opinion that he was waylaid by someone and is being detained against his will.

Detective officers have been specially detailed to inquire at boarding and lodging houses and hotels in various parts of North London in an effort to try and find him.

They are still hoping that Beale may effect his escape from the clutches of whoever is detaining him.

SYBIL THORNDIKE IN
CAR SMASH

Actress Badly Shaken,
But Uninjured

ADEN, Monday.

An hour or so after landing here from the liner Oronsay, Dame Sybil Thorndike, her husband, Mr. Lewis Casson, and son were sight-seeing when the car skidded and overturned. All were badly shaken but uninjured.—Reuter.

HANDCUFFED MAN
CAUGHT

Re-arrested After Vain
Comb-Out of London

Edward Vaughan Barraclough, who escaped from a warder's charge at Charing Cross Station, London, on Friday, was re-arrested at Bushy, Herts, to-day.

Police had combed London for Barraclough, who succeeded in filing off his handcuffs soon after eluding his guard.

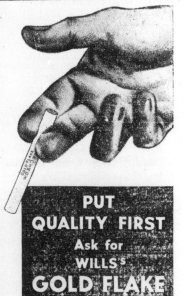

1932

MONDAY APRIL 18TH

Jean Harlow at the Empire City in *The Platinum Blonde*—bargain price seats at 3d, 6d and 7d—Marlene Dietrich in *Dishonoured* at The Stoll Picture Theatre in Bedminster and Greta Garbo in *The Rise Of Helga* at the Regent in Castle Street.

A complete three piece sports suit for just 25s from Shepherds of Clarence Road, your dining room and bedroom fully furnished for 3s 9d weekly by Kerr's of Redcliff Street and luncheons at St Stephen's restaurant in Baldwin Street for 2s and dinners for 3s 6d.

That was life in 1932 . . . the day before Budget Day and two days after Bristol played a dull goalless draw against Stoke. "The fourteenth game played by the City this season in which the Bristol club failed to score yet the vagaries of professional football are such that the players got a bonus of a pound apiece for their successful failing" wrote Half Back.

Mr Chamberlain looked unlikely to offer good news in the next day's Budget . . . and good news was badly needed to lift spirits in the Depression.

"Taxpayers are awaiting with keen anticipation tomorrow's Budget, and various sections are hoping for some alleviation of their burdens. Many hopes, it is to be feared, however, may be dashed".

In Bristol the anticipation was keener still and no hopes were dashed when the cheers rang out in Silver Street.

Day One, *Bristol Evening Post* No 1 and the paper looked a hit from the moment it appeared on the streets of the city.

The crowds outside the Silver Street headquarters who snatched the first copies the moment the newsboys ran out, the excitement at the news-stands and in the newsagents' shops when the Post first appeared and the look and feel of the paper felt right.

Everyone knew the *Evening Post* for what it was. It was the good old *Times and Mirror* with the same staff, the same layout and the same appeal.

The line under the smart new *Bristol Evening Post* masthead read: 'The Paper You Have So Eagerly Awaited'. It would shortly read 'The Paper All Bristol Asked For And Helped To Create', still carried in the Post 60 years later. It might have read, Welcome Back The Paper You Always Loved.

Day One carried two pages of tributes wishing the venture well. The Lord Mayor of Bristol, John H. Inskip, put it clearly enough.

"'Every Bristolian is greatly interested in the birth of their new evening paper, or, rather, in the revival of an old friend which we shall all welcome.' "

And the editor's first editorial column boasted: "Being owned, directed and produced by men of the West—the vast proportion of them born and bred in Bristol—we believe no one can rightly claim that he or she should be able to appreciate and share so entirely the feelings, aspirations and desires of our fellow citizens or so thoroughly supply their needs".

The *Evening Post* had arrived.

1933

TUESDAY JANUARY 31ST

The Post's front page was dominated by one story—the crisis in Australia.

'Australia's Full Reply To MCC—Unnecessary To Cancel Tour—Committee Appointed To Consider "Body Line" Bowling Question.'

The sports story of the season came as a welcome relief to the news from Europe and it gave the paper a chance to brighten up page one at an anxious time.

One much darker event than the Body Line row was foremost in most people's minds that Tuesday, and by the time the Post's first edition appeared on the streets, the paper had had time to mull over events in Germany the day before—and to give the Post's view on the rise to power of a new figure on a troubled world scene.

Ex-House Decorator

"The appointment of Adolf Hitler, an Austrian who was a former house decorator, to the German chancellorship is one of the most spectacular events in modern politics.

"Some 10 years ago his efforts as an agitator got him into trouble with the German Government and it almost appeared his star had set. Released after a brief imprisonment, however, he agitated more fiercely than before and has now almost achieved his ambitions to the full, for he has made no secret of the fact that one day he intends to be president.

"Herr Hitler, who leads the strongest party in the Reichstag and obtained nearly one third of over 35,000,000 votes in the last election, now has the opportunity to demonstrate that he can be something more than an agitator and orator. He has a chance to show he is at least a Mussolini.

"Foreign states, and particularly France, will watch the sequel with some anxiety. Though France appears to have accepted the appointment of Hitler as Chancellor with calmness, Paris was taken by surprise by the suddenness of the happening and already there is a feeling that more difficulties can be expected in Franco-German relations.

"Yet there is reason in the French view that now Hitler is in power his hectic demands for all kinds of reform in foreign affairs will be kept under control by Von Papen and others in the Cabinet.

"The results of his Chancellorship can alone show whether Hitler is a constructive power or is merely a man of sound and fury.

"The communists have already declared war on him and the first 24 hours of his 'reign' did not close before there had been fatal clashes between the communists and his troops. It is obvious that whatever emerges, quiet days for Germany are not just yet."

HITLER BECOMES GERMAN CHANCELLOR
President Von Hindenburg Gives Way To Solve Political Tangle In Berlin

VON PAPEN AS
VICE-CHANCELLOR

1934

MONDAY NOVEMBER 26TH

The Caring Prince, they called him, and the two-year-old *Evening Post* gave blanket coverage to the visit by the Prince of Wales, Prince Edward.

Here was a man who wasn't content just to shake hands with bigwigs and dignitaries. He insisted on meeting His people, the poor, the out-of-work, those hardest hit by the Depression.

The Post followed his footsteps and that night's final edition carried two pages of pictures and a step-by-step account of the day the handsome, dashing Prince came to town.

At the University Settlement's Venture Club for the unemployed in Barton Hill:

"He saw examples of their workmanship including tables and wireless cabinets, rug making, cleverly designed coloured posters and the decoration of metal trays with enamel.

"'I like that very much' the Prince said, grasping one of the trays to give it closer inspection and at once finding his fingers adhering to the sticky surface.

"He burst into laughter and said: 'This is what happens when you touch wet paint'.

"'It is true blue, anyway' called one of the men.

"In conversation he expressed satisfaction that employment was a little better this year and remarked that Bristol had the advantage of having so many industries whereas bad times were especially hard in a place where there was only one industry."

Then to the Dings in St Philips Marsh.

"A large crowd which had gathered at a convenient vantage point at the end of Dings Walk gave a rousing cheer as his car came near.

"The Prince showed evident interest in the houses and first talked to occupiers who were waiting at their front gates.

"He went into Mr H.J. Jenkins' house at 7 Dings Walk and saw the living room. He told Mr Jenkins it was a nice place. The Prince was informed that the houses had baths, in reply to his queries.

"Mrs Jenkins was asked how many children she had and replied there were two who were at school. Mr Jenkins is an unemployed man.

"A visit was paid to Mr and Mrs G.H. Poole at Number 8. The Prince was told that Mr Poole's wages were £2 6s a week and he had three children and the Royal visitor inquired as to how he managed to keep going.

"Mr Poole replied that he lived to the best of his ability. Mr Poole said the Prince remarked it was hard lines in the circumstances."

Then to Knowle and the new council

The Prince of Wales talking to occupants of new housing in the Dings.

housing estate built as part of Bristol's slum clearance scheme. Hundreds of cheering schoolchildren lined Broad Walk.

"The Prince, smoking a pipe, leaned forward in the car and waved his acknowledgement.

"With characteristic thoroughness, the Prince proceeded to inspect one of the Corporation's model houses, 4 Lurgan Walk occupied by Mr and Mrs William G. Bailey and their family of eight, the eldest of whom is 13, the youngest nine months.

"The Prince inspected every room in the house. Mr Bailey, an unemployed builder's labourer, was asked by the Prince how long he had been out of work. 'Eight months, sir' replied Mr Bailey.

"The Prince expressed the hope that Mr Bailey would find employment again.

"Mrs Bailey, who was carrying her youngest child in her arms, was highly delighted by the Prince's visit.

"She said to an Evening Post reporter: 'The Prince soon put us at ease. He asked how I liked living in a council house and I told him we were comfortable indeed. He then asked us how much rent we paid and I was able to tell him we paid less than when we lived in a slum district.' "

1935

When the winter mists came down and mingled on still nights with Bristol's polluted air, it could produce the fatal recipe of fog and smog.

The city's homes, rich and poor, were warmed by open coal fires which sent smoke spiralling up the thickets of chimneys above every street. The factories belched out great clouds of smoke to add to the haze.

Natural mist and still weather joined this man-made cloud to create a blinding fog that was so filthy that a white handkerchief worn mask-like over the mouth to protect the lungs would be stained within minutes.

And so dense could the fog become that it was common for a pedestrian to become completely disorientated even crossing his own road.

The fog came down with a vengeance the night of December 20th and 21st as Bristolians had been preparing for Christmas.

The Post's dramatic front page report of a drowning, rescues and accidents began:

"The worst fog for 50 years . . . the coldest night of a severe winter . . . chaos on road and rail . . . the Christmas trade cut down . . . Mails late . . . a procession of injured at the hospitals.

"That is the weather story to be told today.

"An amazing succession of rescues—and one tragedy—occurred in Bristol Harbour during the night.

"Five men, lost in the fog, fell into the icy water. One, Mr J.B. Norris (19) a bus conductor of Nailsea Close, Bedminster Down, was drowned. Another man who fell in the dock at Avonmouth was rescued.

"A splash and a cry for help revealed the tragedy which befell the young bus conductor. It is thought that after having a cup of tea, he groped through the fog towards his bus and fell over the quayside.

"Directly the alarm was given, fellow employees dashed to the quayside and made desperate efforts to locate him.

"A lifebuoy was thrown in the hope that he might be able to seize it and a life hook was used. With the help of electric torches the police succeeded in finding Norris. Artificial respiration was tried but it was unavailing.

"While taking part in the rescue Mr T.M. Harrison, a bus driver, fell over the quayside. He was rescued within minutes. He was thrown a lifebuoy and was able to grasp it.

"Mr Arthur Lifton (50) of Dongola Road, Bishopston, had an amazing escape when he fell into the harbour after leaving his car near the Cooperative Wholesale Society's premises on Broad Quay.

"He pulled up his car a very short distance from the edge and when he got out, apparently to see where he was, he fell in.

"Luckily he could swim and he managed to make his way to one of the chains hanging from the quay and he was pulled out by the ferryman and another man.

"The fourth man who fell into the harbour was Mr William Morgan (51) of St John's Lane, Bedminster.

"Mr Morgan, who is employed at Bristol Aeroplane Works at Filton, got off the Filton tram at the Tramways Centre, walked towards Prince Street and losing his bearings, found himself in the water.

"Though not a good swimmer, he managed to keep afloat and shouted, with the result that someone threw him a lifebuoy, only just in time. He was rescued by the River Police who rushed to the spot in their launch and took him to the

General Hospital.

"Another who fell in was Mr T. Giles of Castle Street, Trowbridge.

"He had parked his lorry and was directing another driver by Y and Z sheds on Canons Marsh when he walked over the edge of the quayside wall.

"Fortunately he is a strong swimmer and was able to keep afloat. After swimming for some minutes he found an iron ring on the quay wall to which he clung until he was rescued."

1936

FRIDAY DECEMBER 11TH

Britain Enters New Era Of History, the Post announced in a heading above the day's five-strong stack of front page headlines announcing the story of the year.

King Edward had renounced his title to become, at least for the moment, plain Mr Windsor.

The Duke of York would be King George VI. The British monarchy had been turned upside-down in just a few days.

The Post had reported the mounting crisis over King Edward's attempts to marry Mrs Simpson and keep the throne. Now it was all over following Prime Minister Stanley Baldwin's announcement that he would move an Abdication Bill. Edward was leaving for exile in France where he would rejoin his lover.

The Post's Blackboy's diary reported the mood of people . . . and a hectic time at the paper's headquarters in Silver Street, just off Broadmead.

"One has to go back to the General Strike of 10 years ago to find anything approaching the depression which seemed to settle over the whole city before the Prime Minister's statement yesterday.

"When the crisis was first disclosed a week ago, Bristol, in common with other places, seemed to be too stunned to sift the facts and then to form an opinion.

"In many quarters men expressed a great reluctance to discuss the question at all. By tacit consent, the subject was not mentioned.

"Yesterday, however, opinion hardened rapidly.

"Yesterday's demand for the Evening Post recalled that memorable day in 1932 when the paper appeared on the streets of Bristol for the first time.

"Yesterday's large sale of newspapers has to be set against the suspension and cancellation of national advertising due to the uncertainty of the situation.

"The only people who can reasonably be expected to have reaped a real harvest are the newsboys."

And it was the "King has abdicated, Long live the King . . . and the new Queen."

Queen Elizabeth won special praise from Bristol's ex-Mayoress Mrs C.T. Budgett when she talked to an *Evening Post* reporter that day.

She told one of the very first tales that would become part of the legend of the woman who was to be Britain's most popular Royal of them all, the Queen Mum.

"Mrs Budgett recalled the happy incident when the new King and Queen visited the Royal Show at Ashton in Bristol on July 1st and the then Duchess handed a sum of

BRISTOL
EVENING POST

THE PAPER ALL BRISTOL ASKED FOR & HELPED TO CREATE, OUR ASSET IS YOUR GOOD WILL

No. 1,445   FRIDAY, DECEMBER 11 1936.   ONE PENNY

32 PAGES LAST

BRITAIN ENTERS NEW ERA OF HISTORY

The Duke of York Becomes King After Passing of Abdication Act

KING EDWARD WAITED IN SECLUSION TO HEAR NEWS

STROLL AT FORT BELVEDERE AND TALKS WITH SERVANTS

NOW "MR. WINDSOR"

CROWDS OUTSIDE RESIDENCE OF NEW MONARCH

TO-DAY THE BRITISH NATION ENTERED UPON A NEW ERA OF HISTORY. AT 1.52 P.M. THE ROYAL ASSENT WAS SIGNIFIED TO THE ABDICATION BILL, AND AT THAT MOMENT EDWARD THE EIGHTH CEASED TO BE KING. HE BECAME PLAIN MR. EDWARD WINDSOR.

The Attorney-General stated in the House of Commons that there was no compulsion on King Edward to leave the country. *(Full story Page 7.)* To-morrow afternoon the new King will be proclaimed at St. James's Palace.

King Edward VIII. awaited in quiet seclusion at Fort Belvedere the news of the passing of the new Act which ended his short reign, and provided for the accession of the Duke of York.

King Edward took the opportunity of talking to those faithful members of the staff who have served him for many years, and had a look round the house.

To-night, the King, as "Mr. Windsor," will broadcast at 10 o'clock, and the whole world will be listening-in.

London was calm to-day. Many people wandered to the places where lived some of the principal figures in this historical drama.

The Countess of Strathmore, mother of the Duchess of York, entered 145, Piccadilly, by the garden entrance and spent some time with her daughter. Princess Elizabeth accompanied her grandmother to the garden gate, and a nurse saw the Countess into her car.

(Continued on Back Page)

TO-DAY'S EVENTS

9.30—Sir Eric Mieville, Duke of York's Private Secretary, called at the Duke's home in Piccadilly.
10.30—Archbishop of Canterbury visited Marlborough House.
10.50—Mr. Baldwin left 10 Downing Street, for House of Commons.
11.15—Mr. Baldwin moved second reading of Abdication Bill.
11.45—Duke of Kent arrived at Fort Belvedere.
1. 0—Mr. Winston Churchill lunched with King Edward and Duke of Kent at Fort Belvedere.
1.52—Abdication Bill received Royal Assent.

WHERE WILL HE GO?

Mystery of the King's Destination

THE Evening Post understands that when King Edward leaves this country to-night after his final broadcast, he will not go out of Europe.

Plans for his departure are being kept absolutely secret at his own wish.

His destination, too, is a close secret, which will only be revealed after he has left England.

The position of King Edward after his abdication, it was pointed out in authoritative quarters to-day, is not affected by the fact that he is a Knight of the Garter and of other orders of chivalry.

In Denmark it is thought he will stay at Bjornegaard, the estate of Princess Erik, near Holbaek, North-West Zealand. He went there when in Copenhagen for the British Exhibition.

It is also rumoured in Denmark that the King will spend Christmas at Fuen Island, the estate of Count Wedell, a personal friend.

In the Argentine it is reported, without confirmation, that he negotiated for an estate in the Central Argentine district known as the home of Argentine polo.

MRS. SIMPSON

A Reuter Cannes message says: No change has been made in Mrs. Simpson's plans, and no arrangements have been made for a meeting between her and King Edward.

Mrs. Simpson is in excellent health, and does not contemplate leaving Cannes before the end of the year. Lord Brownlow stated that when he left Cannes he would see the King in London unless he had already left.

Great interest was aroused by the publication in a Rome newspaper of a photograph of a motor-car standing in one of the squares of Rome bearing the registration mark of C.U.L. 947, which is the number of the motor-car belonging to Mrs. Simpson in which she made her now historic journey across France to Cannes in company with Lord Brownlow and two detectives.

KING EDWARD on the occasion of a previous broadcast.

A missionary play entitled "The Fires Goes Out" was produced last night by members of Frampton Cotterell Wesleyan Chapel at Thornbury Methodist Chapel. The play is being given on other nights this week at Olveston, Oldbury, and Frampton Cotterell, to raise funds for missionary purposes.

Mainly Fair

S.W. England—Light or moderate southerly winds, veering north-west later; rain at first, fair periods later, occasional rain at first; average day temperature; frost likely at night.

Further Outlook—Mainly fair.

STOP PRESS

PREMIER SEES THE KING.
Mr. Baldwin visited the new King this afternoon, and was busily closeted.

money collected in the Royal Box to an exhibitor who had had £9 10s stolen from him.

"The exhibitor was Mr Davis who had been working as a clogger for over 50 years.

"He had just been fitting the Duchess with a pair of clogs for her to walk around in the mud and she had been most charming to him when the Duchess of Beaufort told her the man had had £9 10s stolen from him.

"The Duchess immediately suggested a collection should be made for the man and asked the Duke of Beaufort to give her his hat. He did so and she walked around the Royal box begging contributions.

"Everyone present put a note into the hat and the money was soon made up.

"The man was called to the Royal Box and the Duchess of York presented the money to him and with the most charming smile told him she hoped he would have better luck with it than he had had with the last.

"The Duchess added: 'You presented me with a beautiful pair of sandals which are very comfortable. I present you with money equal to the sum you have lost.' "

The Duke of Windsor renounced the throne of Britain to marry the woman of his choice.

1937

SATURDAY, NOVEMBER 6TH

The cinema reigned supreme in Bristol in 1937 and even the city's biggest theatre, the Hippodrome on the Centre, had been converted into a sumptuous "picture palace" for the hundreds of thousands of film fans who flocked to the beloved "flicks" at least once a week.

There were two kinds of cinema. There was the 'local', and almost every neighbourhood in Bristol could boast its own picture house with its week-long programme of the main feature film, a B movie, a newsreel, screen advertising and a thrilling trailer tempting film fans to make a date for the next week's attraction.

Then there were the bigger, smarter cinemas in the centre of town. They were the ones which tended to snap up the best of the new Hollywood releases first . . . and so charged customers that little bit more for the privilege of seeing the new Clark Gable, Bette Davis or Gary Cooper movie first.

A night out at the central cinemas meant hopping on a tram or bus from the suburbs, a thrilling evening of screen entertainment and then a return journey on a bus or tram full of other pleasure-seekers chatting about the entertainment they'd just seen.

The movies ruled the roost and each Saturday's *Evening Post* had a full page of film news, of reviews and a full, up-to-the-minute, film-by-film guide of what was on offer for the following seven days "On Bristol's Broadway".

On Saturday, November 6th Bristol's own Cary Grant took starring role on the film page.

The Post's movie correspondent wrote:

"Bristol's film star Cary Grant is in the news.

"He had intended to take a vacation at Tokyo, travelling incognito with his friend and stand-in Mel Merrihue, but the Far Eastern crisis has caused him to change his mind.

"Instead he may go to the Bahamas or to Rio de Janeiro.

"Cary's current release *For You Alone* comes to the Regent Cinema on November 15. In this merry musical he appears with opera star Grace Moore.

"He has been cast opposite a number of singers, including Irene Dunne, in his 23 screen productions.

"It is stated that he has been signed for another role with Katherine Hepburn in her next starring feature, *Bringing Up Baby*.

"Cary, who recently completed *Topper and The Awful Truth*, supports Miss Hepburn in *Sylvia Scarlett*."

And from that day's "On Bristol's Broadway", some of the current releases to be seen in town:

Bristol Hippodrome: *The Show Goes On* (U). "Gracie Fields as a millgirl singer who reaches for the top."

Empire, Triangle; *On The Avenue* (U). "A real treat of songs, dances, fun, romance. Dick Powell, Alice Faye, Madeleine Carroll and the Ritz Brothers."

Embassy: *Prince And The Pauper* (A). "Fate made one lad a king and the other a beggar. Erroll Flynn, Claud Rains . . . spectacular."

Stoll, Bedminster: *Platinum Blonde* (U). "The star the world mourned in the role that made her famous. Jean Harlow and Loretta Young."

Ambassador, Winterstoke Road: *Gold Diggers Of 1937* (U). "Dick Powell, Joan Blondell and Glenda Farrell in a bright musical show with romance and fun."

Carlton, Westbury: *A Day At The Races* (U). "The Marx Brothers in one of their funniest comedies."

1938

THURSDAY JUNE 2ND

His pals called him Dare because of his recklessness . . . and 17-year-old Albert Gourd lived up to his reputation in a spectacular manner in the skies over Bristol that night.

The teenager chose a clear summer's evening to scramble out of a plane flying over Bristol and free-fall and then parachute his way down to a bumpy landing on a Clifton roof-top watched by tens of thousands of anxious onlookers below.

" 'I put my feet on the cockpit and sat on the back for a minute to get used to the feel of the air. The plane, about 4,000 feet up, was travelling at between 120 and 160 miles an hour and the rush of air was terrific.

" 'Then I went over the port side head first. The rush of the propeller carried me down and behind the tail of the machine.

" 'When I had fallen to about 1,500 feet I could see people running about in all directions shouting and wondering where I was coming down. I would have liked to have come down in the Centre if it had not been for the live wires.'

"That is part of a remarkable story told to the Evening Post today by Albert Gourd, 17, of Easton Road, Bristol who thousands of people saw leap from an aeroplane whilst it was flying high over the Avon Gorge at about 8 o'clock last night.

"At first they could only identify what looked like a black object falling from the machine.

"It dropped sheer for some hundreds of feet, then a parachute opened and they saw suspended from it a man.

"In the strong breeze he was carried quickly over the city.

"Motorists dashing after in pursuit saw him dropping towards the university.

"Suddenly he seemed to swoop downwards and was lost to sight. People in Park Row saw him descending rapidly. He skimmed the roofs and landed between two houses in Woodland Road.

"Rushing to the spot, they found the parachute entangled in the chimney stack of No 86 and the parachutist hanging by the ropes down the side of the house."

The daredevil was rescued by a man who found a builder's ladder, climbed up and unhitched the teenager from his 'chute. The 17-year-old calmly climbed down the ladder, nodded to the astonished onlookers . . . and lit up a cigarette before leaving.

The Post was quickly on to the story and tracked him down, discovering that young Gourd worked in the building trade and was, in his spare time, serving with the Reserves in 501 Bombing Squadron based at Filton. That was how he'd managed to get airborne.

The lad told the Post's man:

" 'I was flying in a Hawker Hart piloted by Flying Officer Rayner and occupying the air gunner's seat.

" 'There was nothing the matter with the aeroplane when I jumped. I did it for bravado. The pilot did not know anything about it, you bet!

" 'I was not scared. I have not been scared about anything that I can remember except having two teeth cut. My nickname is Dare because I am usually ready to dare anything. I have been in hospital several times as a result of escapades.' "

THAT is part of the remarkable ~~story of~~ ... story told to the Evening Post to-day by Albert Gourd, the 17-year-old youth of 141, Easton Road, Bristol, who thousands of people saw leap from an aeroplane while it was flying high above the Avon Gorge at about 8 o'clock last night.

At first they could only identify what looked like a black object falling from the machine.

It dropped sheer for some hundreds of feet, then a parachute opened and they saw suspended from it a man.

In the strong breeze he was carried quickly over the city.

Motorists dashed off in pursuit, and saw him dropping towards the University.

Suddenly he seemed to swoop downwards and was lost to sight.

People in Park Row and neighbourhood saw him descending rapidly. He skimmed the roofs and dropped between two houses in Woodland Road.

Rushing to the spot, they saw the parachute entangled in the chimney stack of No. 86, and the parachutist the air gunner's seat.

"There was nothing the matter with the aeroplane when I jumped, and I did it for bravado.

"The pilot did not know anything about it, you bet. I had previously told people that I was going to do it, and they were constantly picking me up that I had not done it.

"I had only been up once before, and then for only five minutes. This time I had been in the air exactly four minutes.

"When I jumped I decided that before I pulled the parachute cord I was going to count three, but I think I counted two very slowly. I was falling at a rate of 120 feet a second, so I should have fallen about 240 feet when I pulled the cord.

WHEN HE WAS SCARED

"Nothing happened for a moment, and I got the usual feeling of ' will it, or won't it.' I kept falling, and then it opened with a terrific jerk, almost like breaking every bone in one's body, and I am still covered with bruises from the harness.

"But I was not scared; in fact, I have

GERMA
SPAIN SH

Statement a
Confere

MR. J. C. Little, the Amalgama Union, produced part gun belt, containing tured from Franco's to the National Co Union at Morecambe

"If you look at the m "you will see that they many."

Mr. Little declared Government military le "If your people would Hurricane chasers we Franco's bombing."

AIR-RAID " WEL(

Mr. Little was speak instructing the execut organised efforts to Government into recog national rights of the ment.

He described how a delegation with which Barcelona was welcome an air raid, and said he the front line himself bu would be more useful in

The National Commit up a voluntary levy fund lorries for the Spanish member to be invited shilling a month with of raising £50,000.

Countess Waldegrave fete arranged by the Y.W.C.A., at Southmead Road, Bristol, at 3 p June 18.

Holder of the British speed record, an L.M touched 114 m.p.h. on of the Coronation Sc honoured by the King will make his last trip this week-end. He is Clarke, of Crewe, who ing British railway spe a year ago.

AN EXCLUSIVE EVENING POST picture of Albert Gourd (left) taken immediately after landing in Woodland Road. A friend in the background is seen carrying the parachute to a waiting car.

hanging by the ropes down the side of the house.

By wonderful good fortune he found a foothold on the snow box of a waterpipe leading down from the roof, and thus took the weight off the fabric of the parachute.

CLIMBED LADDER

Someone with ready wit bethought themselves of a builder's ladder at the University Science wing extensions at the top of Woodland Road. Ready hands assisted to hurry it to the scene.

The parachutist, showing amazing unconcern, grasped the rungs, swung round it, and descended to the ground, undamaged beyond a scratch on the leg and never been scared of anything that I can remember, except having two teeth out. I fell very fast after the 'chute opened, as the wind was so strong. Immediately the pilot missed me he made for the drome, and lorries were soon out searching for me.

"I was glad to pass over the Avon clear of the mud, and I also was very thankful to pass several rather sharp steeples!

"After all, one does value one's life, even if one does not mind getting knocked about a bit, as I do not.

"My nickname among my pals is ' Dare.' because I am usually ready to dare anything, and have been in hospital several times as results of escapades.

"The possibility of my getting knocked

some good time cycling from Easton to Westo Ashton. I go in for e on which I can lay my fit and always willing to

In his fall Mr. Gourd roof shuting of the ho Road.

The pilot of the plane got back to Filton that that his passenger had le he felt its balance distu

MOTHER'S AGON

What was presumably

BRISTOL
EVENING POST
LAST

THE PAPER ALL BRISTOL ASKED FOR & HELPED TO CREATE : OUR ASSET IS YOUR GOOD WILL

No. 2,293   MONDAY, SEPTEMBER 4 1939.   ONE PENNY

TORPEDO SINKS BRITISH LINER

Hundreds of Americans Among the 1,400 on Board

MANY PICKED UP FROM BOATS

CAPTAIN'S RADIO MESSAGE REVEALS DEATHS IN EXPLOSION

THE ATHENIA.

DESTROYERS' DASH

THE British liner Athenia (13,581 tons), outward bound to Canada with 1,400 passengers and crew, has been torpedoed and sunk in the Atlantic.

Donaldson Atlantic Line, Ltd., the owners, have received the following radio message from Captain Cook, the master :

"Torpedoed 250 miles west of Inishtrahull (an island off the north coast of Donegal). Passengers and crew, except those killed by explosion, taken to boats and picked up by various ships."

More than 300 Americans were in the Athenia, and it is stated that officials at the White House heard the news with obvious feelings of horror.

RULES VIOLATED

The Ministry of Information state that the Athenia was torpedoed without warning at least 200 miles from land—"action which is in direct contravention of the rules regarding submarine warfare, by which Germany is bound."

Destroyers have been sent off at full speed to help in picking up the survivors.

Late this afternoon it was reported that the Swedish yacht Southern Cross had picked up 200 of the Athenia's passengers, and 800 others are stated to have been saved by the Norwegian steamer Knute Nelson.

SINKING OF LUSITANIA RECALLED

MR. Joseph P. Kennedy, the U.S. Ambassador, has called all the information in his possession to Washington.

Mr. Stephen Early, secretary to President Roosevelt, said:

"I should like to point out that according to official information the ship had come from Glasgow to Liverpool and was bound for Canada, bringing refugees.

"I point this out to show that there was no possibility, according to official information, that the ship was carrying any munitions or anything of that kind." It is officially stated that the Athenia took on board 145 United States passengers at Glasgow and 65 at Belfast on Friday.

Children on Board

A number of children were among those who embarked at Belfast. Ten college girls who had cut short a holiday in Scotland to get home quickly were also on board.

Sir Richard (Stuart) Lake, a former Lieutenant-Governor of Saskatchewan, and Lady Lake are stated by friends to be passengers.

Captain James Reid, marine superintendent of Donaldson Atlantic Line, Ltd., told the Evening Post that he believed a large

and another 103 at Liverpool on Saturday. She left Liverpool at 4 p.m.—19 hours before war broke out.

MR. CHAMBERLAIN BROADCASTS TO GERMANY

HIS STATEMENT REPEATED AT INTERVALS

FOLLOWING is the text of Mr. Chamberlain's talk to the German people, first broadcast at 1.15 yesterday afternoon and repeated at intervals since :—

"German people,—Your country and mine are now at war. Your Government has asked and invaded the free and independent State of Poland, which this country is in honour bound to defend.

"Because your troops were not withdrawn in response to the Note which the British Government addressed to the German Government, war has followed.

"With the horrors of war we are familiar. God knows this country has done everything possible to prevent this calamity. But now that the invasion of Poland by Germany has taken place it has become inevitable.

THE FACTS

"You are told by your Government that you are fighting because Poland rejected your leader's offer and resorted to arms.

"What are the facts ? The so-called 'offer' was made to the Polish Ambassador in Berlin on Thursday evening two hours before the announcement by your Government that it had been 'rejected.'

"So far from having been rejected there had been no time even to consider it. Your Government had previously demanded that a Polish representative should be sent to Berlin within 24 hours to conclude an agreement.

"At that time the 16 points subsequently put forward had not even been communicated to the Polish Government.

"A DICTATE"

"The Polish representative was expected to arrive within a fixed time to sign an agreement which he had not even seen. This is not negotiation. This is a dictate.

"To such methods no self-respecting and powerful State could assent. Negotiations on a free and equal basis might well have settled the matter in dispute.

"You may ask why Great Britain is concerned. We are concerned because we gave our word of honour to defend Poland against aggression.

"Why did we feel it necessary to pledge ourselves to defend this Eastern Power when our interests lie in the West, and when your Leader has said he has no interest in the west ?

"The answer is that—and I regret to have to say it—that nobody in this country any longer places any trust in your Leader's word.

He gave his word that he would respect the Locarno Treaty; he broke it.

BOLSHEVISM'S ALLY

"He gave his word that he neither wished nor intended to annex Austria; he broke it.

(Continued on Back Page.)

Poles Claim To Have Retaken Five Towns

CROSS INTO GERMAN TERRITORY IN PURSUIT OF ENEMY

RECAPTURE of five towns is claimed by Poland, while Germany reports advances of her troops in the south-west and near the southern border of Danzig territory. Warsaw states that 1,500 persons were killed in air raids during the first two days of the war.

ON LAND

While it is officially admitted in Warsaw that the town of Czestochowa, the "Polish Lourdes," has had to be abandoned, Polish cavalry have, it is claimed, reoccupied ten towns on the Western front, and gains are reported from the East Prussian front.

Earlier reports from Warsaw had stated that Czestochowa, which lies about 17 miles from the Upper Silesian frontier, was burning as the result of German air raids.

The towns recaptured by Polish cavalry units are Lesno and Rawitz, which were seized by the Germans on Friday.

The Polish troops afterwards crossed into German territory in pursuit of the enemy.

The Poles have also reoccupied the frontier town of Strasil, which was occupied by the Germans on the night of August 31-September 1, without a fight.

A COMMUNIQUE

A communique issued by the Polish General Staff last night stated :

"Land operations.—Stubborn attacks on the front of Sierdz and Pultusk (Tatra Mountains) continue. Strong armoured groups have been seen near Czestochowa.

"The evacuation of the town has begun.

"In face of enemy forces several times superior and a big quantity of armoured units, of heavy artillery, and aviation, our armies have been obliged to retreat in silence.

"On the East Prussian front fighting continues at the frontier as well as in the region of Danzig and Gdynia, where we have recovered Orlowo and Puck.

"Westerplatte—at the entrance to Danzig harbour—continues to be defended."

The Warsaw broadcasting station reports German parachute jumpers alighted behind the Polish lines in Silesia and endeavouring to cut telephone and telegraphic connections and damage communications.

BERLIN CLAIMS

Meanwhile Berlin claims the capture of two other towns in addition to Czestochowa.

These are Radomsko, north of the industrial region round Katowitz, and about 40 miles from the Polish frontier, and Dzia-

FRANCE IN ACTION

PARIS, Monday.
France's first war communique issued here to-day stated :

"Operations have been begun by the whole land, sea, and air forces."

IN THE AIR

Owing to low clouds, German aerial activity over Warsaw has diminished. Two columns of German tanks on the march near Czestochowa are dispersed by Polish aircraft with heavy losses. The Poles lost four planes.

A communique issued by the Polish General Staff last night says: "Attacks of

German aviation on Polish territory continued throughout the day (yesterday). There have been heavy losses among the civilian population.

"On September 2 Warsaw, Deblin, Radomish, Torun, and Cracow were bombed.

"German planes bombed numerous

(Continued on Back Page.)

1939

MONDAY SEPTEMBER 4TH

It was the first full day of the war following Prime Minister Neville Chamberlain's radio announcement that black Sunday.

Theatres closed, cinemas were shut, motorists were warned once again that their headlights must be dimmed to the lowest light possible.

The drama company due to stage the play *The Corn Is Green* at the Prince's Theatre in Park Row, arrived in Bristol the night before and then left for London.

"At the Bristol Hippodrome, the scenery for the new musical show *I Can Take It* arrived at the end of last week. The company, including the stars Jessie Matthews and Sonnie Hale, have not left London, although the scenic staff were in possession of the theatre at the weekend.

"Patrons who booked seats for the show in advance are asked to note that the money will be refunded to them as soon as sanction for the repayment has been obtained from head office."

And the blackout came . . . and stayed.

"Although there was some improvement in the "blackout" in Bristol last night, the Chief Constable, Mr C.G. Maby, emphasises that it is still very far from satisfactory and much more attention to windows is necessary in order to comply with the regulations which are being strictly enforced.

"'We have found,' said the Chief Constable in a statement today, 'that many people seem to think that the same care is not needed with regard to their rear windows as with those facing the highway.

"'That is an entirely wrong idea. It is important, in their own and the general public interest, that ALL lights should be effectively screened, whether at the back, front or side.

"'We have found, too, that there is a certain laxity in the screening of lights at public houses. Some are adopting measures which are not sufficiently effective.

"'People should also remember that when they open their doors rays of light must not be allowed out.'

"An Evening Post reporter's impression of the black-out last night was that road-users were much at fault, particularly on the highways outside the city. Some were using unobscured sidelights, some fog lamps and some even beam lights without any screening. Many cyclists were seen without shielding on their lamps and some motor-cyclists with lamps as strong as car's beams were particular offenders.

"As was to be expected, there were crashes, but mostly with damage limited to the cars involved. In one, just beyond Redhill, three cars were involved.

"One motorist halted to look for a side turning; another overtaking failed to see the stationary car in time, struck it a glancing blow and went across the road to the verge on the offside and a third car following behind swerved but had a sideways bump, and finished up side by side with the other on the bank.

"Fortunately there were no personal injuries.

"The white centre line is proving a real boon."

Bristol Evening Post, November 25, 1940

RADIO ON PAGE 8

BRISTOL
EVENING POST

LAST

"It's a Grand Life if we Don't Weaken"—Britain's Watchword for the Winter — Picture

No. 2,674   Bristol 20646   MONDAY, NOVEMBER 25 1940.   ONE PENNY

TO BE
OF
EVENING

PLA
REGULAR
ORDER W
NEWSAGENT O

GERMANS CONCENTRATE
ON WEST TOWN

Churches, Theatre, Cinemas, Schools,
Home for Aged, Historic Buildings,
And Shopping and Co

SENATOR
TO URGE
CREDITS

MORE U.S. AID
FOR BRITAIN?

Greeks
Take New
Town

AND 1,500 MORE

R.A.
BOM
RAIL
HAM

A Big
Key

Dock

1940

"The enemy's main attack last night was aimed at a town in the West of England.

"It began shortly after dark and continued until shortly before midnight.

"High explosives and many incendiary bombs were dropped and houses and commercial buildings were damaged by fire and explosions. Some persons were killed and others injured.

"A home for the elderly, at least half a dozen places of worship, a school, a theatre, cinemas, shops, houses and commercial buildings suffered damage by fire and blast.

"A grammar school, a warehouse and some coalyards were also affected.

"Fortunately the people from the home for old people, which was set alight, had been evacuated to a hospital early in the raid.

"At least 50 fires were burning at one time.

"The raiders, flying singly, arrived almost continuously and were fiercely challenged by anti-aircraft batteries.

"Townspeople remained calm throughout the raid and afterwards toured the main streets to see the damage.

"In the early hours of the morning, when men and women and girls streamed to their places of business and work, the same calm courageous spirit was to be seen.

"'I'm tough' declared one girl and certainly that was the quality shown by everyone.

"Shopping streets suffered severely, as did some perfect specimens of ancient and modern architecture and places of historic interest.

"Bombs fell on several thoroughfares, damaging gas mains and setting two alight.

"Having regard to the scale of the attack, the casualties were remarkably light.

"The call on the firemen, regular and auxiliary, was responded to with the greatest quality and assistance was rushed in from neighbouring areas.

"While it would be better to say that not only the fire fighting services but all the air raid defence services worked heroically.

"Working coolly and without pause, unstinted admiration was granted them everywhere.

"A milk bar opened during the height of the attack and although buildings on each side were in flames, the employees handed out hot soup to the firemen and ARP wardens."

The town in the West was Bristol, this was the first great Bristol Blitz and the Post was barred from mentioning its name by the censors.

No pictures of the raid were published until the day afterwards following the censors' decrees and although they showed familiar sights of Bristol reduced to smoking ruins, the captions still described the damage as having happened in "a town in the West Country".

The damage had been severe and casualties were heavy, but the full information was not released until much later.

The raid on the night of Sunday November 24th, 1940 cost 207 lives. Another 187 were seriously injured and a further 703 slightly hurt.

Black-Out time was published nightly in the Post. That Monday the front page blackout panel reminded Bristolians: Blackout starts 5.38 p.m., Ends 8.16 p.m.

1941

SATURDAY APRIL 12TH

Good Friday, 1941, was the last of the six major air raids that marked the Bristol Blitz. The sirens sounded at 9.46 p.m. and for the next two hours bombs fell from a cloudless sky.

An all-clear was sounded after that but it was a false alarm. A second wave of bombers arrived over the city, catching many people out of their shelters and off-guard. The final death toll was 180 with another 146 seriously hurt and 236 slightly injured.

Bristol was not to know it the following morning, but the worst of the war was now over for its citizens.

By coincidence, the Prime Minister, Winston Churchill, saw the blitz from a distance on Good Friday night. He had been arriving for the next day's Degree Congregation at Bristol University, where he was Chancellor, when the bombs started falling. His train was held back until the final all-clear sounded, and then he and his party pulled into town.

"The Prime Minister with the American Ambassador and President Roosevelt's direct representative in connection with the Lease-and-Lend Act, today toured some of Bristol's blitzed areas.

"Mr Churchill, complete with familiar hat and inevitable cigar, left his hotel early today and met the Lord Mayor and Town Clerk at the Council House.

"When the distinguished visitors and civic officials began their tour, the news spread quickly and cheering crowds soon gathered.

"Smiling broadly and standing in an open car, the Prime Minister waved his hat and cigar in acknowledgment.

"He looked very fit and discussed Bristol's ordeal with members of the official party.

"Just as his car turned out of sight, a large crowd of men and women came running towards the Council House waving and cheering breathlessly as accompanying cars started off in its wake.

"In the blitzed areas he was also heartily cheered by people who endured a severe ordeal last night. He replied: 'God bless you'.

"To a man working on repairs to a bombed building, Mr Churchill said: 'Don't worry. We will give it them back'.

"At a place where shelter building was in progress, he told the bricklayers, 'I've done a bit of that', a reference to the time when he made bricklaying a hobby.

"Among those with whom he talked in a residential area was a woman whose house suffered last night.

"Mr Churchill held out his hand but she demurred because her hand was dirty from 'cleaning up'. But the Prime Minister insisted on shaking hands.

"Mr Churchill bought from a sailor one of the emblems—a Union Jack—on sale in aid of Bristol's Own Fund for providing comfort for men in the Services and Civil Defence.

"One of the objects of Mr Churchill's visit was to attend the congregation for the Conferment of Degrees at Bristol University, of which he is Chancellor.

"The congregation was a special one for the conferment of an honorary degree of Doctor of Laws on Mr Menzies, Prime Minister of Australia.

"With Mr Churchill was his wife and their daughter Mary.

"The party arrived in the early hours after the blitz and breakfasted at the Grand Hotel."

The front page footnote gave Black-Out times for ensuring that no lights of any kind were shown from households.

1942

FRIDAY AUGUST 28TH

The great air raids on Bristol were a thing of the past . . . the last had been at Easter, 1941. The Yanks were arriving. The tide was turning.

And then, out of an August morning sky, terror returned to Bristol. Censorship had been largely lifted and the Post's story that day was one of the most vivid accounts of Bristol's war.

"Two raiders came in high and one dropped a bomb on Bristol this morning. It fell at a junction where three buses laden with business people were halted. The casualty list will probably be high.

"The bomb fell among the buses and in a moment two were afire, the occupants being trapped; the other was wrecked. A number of people passing in the street were thrown a considerable distance by the blast.

"A 16th century timbered building, home of a well established printing firm, partially collapsed while an adjacent building was brought down completely.

"It is feared that a number of people are buried in the debris. Ambulances were quickly on the scene and those of the injured who could be extricated were removed to hospital.

"It happened that the terminal for the buses had been transferred to allow street alterations. This accounted for there being three of them on the street while, happening at an hour when traffic is heavy, the number of passengers was greater than would have been the case at other than the peak hour of morning travel.

"The bomb came down without warning so that nobody had time to take shelter. The buses were a mass of flames almost immediately the bomb burst and nothing could be done for the people within. Though the fire brigade were on the spot in force within little more than a minute, they could do little except prevent a spread of the fire to nearby buildings.

"Two had already burst into flames but the fires were quickly got under control. Even as the firemen were playing on the burning debris of the building which had collapsed, others were tearing away beams and bricks in the seemingly vain hope of rescuing workers believed to have been on the premises.

"A press photographer had a lucky escape. He had been on fire watching duties overnight and he was leaving his office to go home when a bus passed him. He ran to catch it but was too late. That bus was involved in the tragedy.

"As the bus passed out of sight round the corner, he heard the sound of the planes overhead followed almost imme-

diately by the unmistakable shriek of a falling bomb.

"It crashed though into a culvert close to the nearest bus while a second bus just ahead of it caught the full blast.

"The third bus, outward bound, was wrecked but did not catch fire. People, seriously injured and some dead, were lying on the road, among them women and children.

"It is believed that the drivers and conductors or conductresses of two of the buses are among the dead.

"Aboard one of the buses, in which a baby was one of the victims, everybody was a casualty with the exception of the conductress who escaped with shock.

"Her first thought was for the driver. 'Is my driver safe?' she asked again and again.

"An eye witness, Mr H. Sheppard, said: 'There was a girl on the rear platform of one of the buses and with another man I rushed up and caught hold of her—but as her foot was trapped and the flames swept up we had to release our hold. The heat was too intense for anyone to be able to do anything.

" 'Another young woman jumped from the top of one of the buses and, I believe, was uninjured.' "

The 500lb bomb, which fell on Broad Weir, was by far the costliest in lives and injuries of any dropped on Bristol. It killed 45, mostly women and children, and injured 56.

1943

SATURDAY JULY 31ST

War or no war, everyone was determined that the August Bank Holiday of 1943 would be one to remember . . . and it was.

The West Country was full of men and women in the uniforms of many nationalities, huge service camps had sprung up in the countryside and the mood in the summer of '43 was one of real optimism after the dark early days of the war. We were going to win.

That holiday weekend saw a happy rush to the coast to enjoy the hot August weather that turned into a stampede.

"Hundreds of people unable to board the packed-like-sardines trains slept for hours on the platforms and in the subway at Temple Meads station last night. Passengers swarmed on every platform.

"Weston-super-Mare was the magnet for a big majority and the 10 a.m. train was so full that in addition to standing in the corridors two deep and with four and five standing in the carriages, the luggage vans were also packed.

"When the next train to Weston came in those who had been left behind surged forward, women with young babies in arms being among those scrambling to get in.

"One woman with a small baby arrived just as the train was starting to move and willing hands seized her and the child and just managed to get her in.

"A railways spokesman said: 'We are beating all records, even for peacetime'.

"The demand for accommodation in the rural districts around Weston is probably heavier than it has ever been. In the Puxton district, more people are staying on farms than ever before."

Servicemen, many of them GIs based in and around Bristol, quickly got into the swing of the August Bank Holiday mood and they flocked to the busy fairs and fetes.

One pretty girl was pictured in the Post "showing her American friend how to swing it at the Durdham Down carnival" aboard a large fairground swing.

And families who couldn't get away from town had plenty to keep them happy.

"Hundreds of people took their 'seaside' holiday at Page Park, Staple Hill. Attractions included donkeys, ponies, sand pits and paddling pools.

"On Frenchay Common there were tugs-of-war, children's sports and a cricket match. The profits will go to the men serving in the forces."

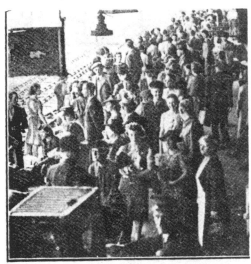

DETERMINED TO TRAVEL.—A section of one of the platforms at Temple Meads last evening.

BRISTOL
EVENING POST

No. 3,766—1½d.   The Paper All Bristol Asked For and Helped to Create   Tues., June 6 1944

ALLIES INVADE FRANCE

'Already Hope that Tactical Surprise has been Attained'—Premier

SEA OBSTACLES NOT SO DIFFICULT AS WERE EXPECTED

Thousands of Ships and 11,000 First Line Allied Planes

MR. Churchill, announcing in the Commons the Allied landings in France, said: "An immense armada of upwards of 4,000 ships, with several thousand smaller craft, have crossed the Channel. So far the commanders who are engaged report that everything is proceeding according to plan—and what a plan.

"Obstacles which were constructed in the sea have not proved so difficult as was apprehended.

"The Anglo-American Allies are sustained by about 11,000 first-line aircraft, which can be drawn upon as may be needed for the purpose of battle.

"There are already hopes that actual tactical surprise has been attained, and we hope to furnish the enemy with a succession of surprises during the course of the fighting."

MASSED AIRBORNE LANDINGS

MR. Churchill, who was greeted with tremendous cheers, first apologised for keeping the House waiting, remarking that questions would rise more rapidly than usual.

None of his statement was so ...

"I have to announce to the House that during the night and the early hours of this morning the first of the series of landings on the Continent of Europe has taken place. In this case the liberating assault first took place on the coast of France."

Vast Plan

He then referred to the armada of ships, the invasion, and added:

"Massed airborne landings have been successfully effected behind the enemy's lines.

"Landings on the beaches are proceeding at various points at the present time. The fire of the shore batteries has been largely quelled ...

... There is complete unity between the Allied commanders.

Second Only To ...

"We are living through momentous hours now. I think the Prime Minister's statement ranks second to the declaration of war ...

AN AIR OBSERVER REPORTS—

Allied Troops Are Slashing Inland

TERRIFIC BOMBING ONSLAUGHT

Photo reconnaissance pilot, report that the Allies have established beach-heads and are slashing inland from the coast of Normandy.

COUNTRYSIDE H.Q.

How "Button" Was Pressed

GEN. Dwight Eisenhower "pressed the button" for the invasion at a camp in the depth of the sleeping English countryside, where, from a motor trailer, he is directing the first phase of history's most gigantic amphibious operation.

It was at night that the Supreme Commander, pink, strong, and confident, made his great decision. Final weather forecasts determined the choice.

The General has had little sleep for many hours, but his stride is fresh and alert between his office on wheels and his war-room with its pregnant maps.

Great Barrage

"The umbrella bombardment from Allied warships began as soon as dawn broke," reports a military observer who landed with the first assault forces.

"It seemed that hell itself had been let loose."

Up the Beaches

"Within a very short space of time the immediate beachhead was clear ..."

LONDON
GLOUCESTER
BRISTOL
BRISTOL CHANNEL
DOVER
CALAIS
ANTWERP
BRUSSELS
BOULOGNE
CHERBOURG
CAEN
ROUEN
LAON
RHEIMS
MAILLY
PARIS
0 MLS 100   200

We Land on Channel Islands

HEAVY Fighting at Caen, 10 Miles Inland, Say Nazis

Allied troops have landed on Guernsey and Jersey, reports the German Overseas News Agency. It adds that tanks have been landed in the area of Arromanches, 10 miles north-east of Bayeux.

GERMAN radio gave the following report of the invasion of the Normandy coast:

"Early this morning numerous landing craft and light warships were observed in the area between the mouth of the Seine and the eastern coast of Normandy, as far as Cherbourg.

"At the same time paratroops were dropped from numerous aircraft on the northern tip of the Normandy Peninsula.

"It is believed that these paratroops have been given the task of capturing airfields in order to facilitate the landing of further paratroops.

"The harbour of Le Havre is, at the moment, being bombarded. German naval forces have engaged enemy landing craft off the coast.

"The long-expected invasion appears to have begun.

"The main centres of the air landing attacks are in the whole of ...

(Continued on Back Page, Col. 4.)

PETAIN FEARS REPRISALS

His Radio Plea For 'Most Rigorous Discipline'

SPEAKING under great emotional stress, Petain broadcast on Paris radio today ...

(Continued on Back Page, Col. 1.)

1944

TUESDAY JUNE 6TH

The great armies of Allied troops which had been encamped in the Bristol region and the rest of the West Country had packed and vanished.

Everyone knew where they had gone. To the South Coast and dockside bases somewhere.

The night sky had been full of aircraft, streaming southwards. Great events were imminent.

And by the morning of June 6th the news had broken. The Allied invasion of Europe had begun with mass landings of troops on the beaches of Normandy.

There was an almost audible sigh of relief that the waiting was over. Now, at last, we were hitting back. The final chapter of World War II had clearly begun.

That day's editorial in the *Evening Post* expressed the mood perfectly:

"The hour has struck. Never in the world's most dramatic annals have the nations of the Earth faced a more grim or thrilling crisis than now unfolds.

"From our own headquarters the first news came in the form of a warning to the people of France. We promised them this warning and the promise has been redeemed. They will understand, for they have not forgotten how they were herded into the roadways by the ruthless Huns in order to impede all military movement when France was attacked and struck down.

"Following swiftly upon this warning came details of where our first blows had struck. Let it not be imagined, however, that the whole story, or anything like the whole story, has yet been unfolded.

"It will be impossible in the early stages to distinguish between operations that are feints and operations that are an integral part of what we all hope will be a victorious march on Berlin.

"Of one thing, however, we may be certain—the offensive commenced in the West will be followed swiftly by a resumed Russian offensive in the East.

"The opening of the campaign has been postponed longer than most of us expected. The reason will be divulged in due course.

"But although there may have been unavoidable delays, nearly six months of fair campaigning weather should still lie ahead of us. We have the right to look forward to those six months with confidence as well as hope.

"No nation has put forward a more supreme effort in preparations for this, the momentous day in the history of the world."

1945

TUESDAY MAY 8TH

"Earlier the momentous news that Germany had completely surrendered had been received without any great outward display of emotion.

"Even after it was known that today would be officially regarded as VE-Day there were few immediate signs of excitement. All seemed to have decided that VE-Day celebrations could not come until the Prime Minister had made his broadcast.

"Almost as soon as the first news of surrender had been received, however, flags began to sprout from many houses and business premises.

"Queen's Road had ropes of them from one side of the thoroughfare to the other, and bunting and pennants festooned the fronts of shops in the windows of many of which were colourful patriotic displays.

"Another area to make a bright show was Mary-le-Port Street where the gay array had as a background many grim reminders of the war in the form of blitz debris.

"The Council House, too, was well beflagged.

"During the evening Bristol became a city of flags. From the business houses, the public buildings and pre-eminently from the homes of the people, decorations were hung.

"Bedminster seemed to set the pace, and although many other districts probably equalled their achievements in the end, nowhere can have excelled them. Ere the evening was out, every Bedminster street had to be entered beneath many arches of flags of all the Allied nations and all the time residents continued to bring out more decorations to add to the grand array.

"In other parts of the city it was largely the same story, if to a lesser degree.

"Children, of course, were everywhere in high spirits. Most of them—and many of their elders too—began wearing red, white and blue favours, some produced hats of similar hue and not a few appeared in fancy-dress summer costume.

"Hawkers at the Centre did a brisk trade in favours and numerous girls, having bought colourful paper hats at a shop in nearby Denmark Street, strolled at The Centre wearing them at jaunty angles.

"At theatres and cinemas when the official news of VE-Day was announced, there were outbursts of cheering and applause.

"At the Theatre Royal, where Mr T. Hickson said he was proud to make the historic announcement from the most historic stage in the country, the audience rose from their seats to applaud.

"Mr Gerald Hornby told the Empire audience at the close of the second house and then led them and the company in the singing of 'Abide With Me', 'Land Of Hope And Glory' and the National Anthem.

"There were scenes of great excitement at the Orpheus Cinema when Mr A.T. Miller interrupted the main feature to give the news while statements by the managers of the King's (Mr R. Cowgill) and the New Palace (Mr R.G.H. Blackburn) were also greeted with tremendous applause.

"There were similar scenes at other cinemas where the announcement was made.

"At the Embassy, Mr J.E. Williams had previously announced surrender news, going on the stage accompanied by two members of the RAF, an American soldier, a British Tommy and a naval officer. Here the audience stood and waved handkerchiefs and papers as they cheered.

"At some cinemas the special Victory trailer film was put on during the last

performance; in many others it was screened today.

"After 10 o'clock, with dusk falling, the entirely unlighted Centre (for the full street lighting was not to be used until VE-night) began to show scenes of greater animation.

"Young men—many in uniform—and girls formed small groups singing popular songs; others with arms linked strolled along the pavement in high spirits; an American soldier and a British girl entertained with a 'jitterbug' dance in the car park and a party formed a circle and danced light-heartedly for some minutes.

"In public-houses all over the city, most of them not unduly full, there was singing.

"Those who, since the dim-out was lifted, have continued to pull their curtains at night, left them undrawn on this occasion so that when darkness descended the hilly part of the city, viewed from the Ashton district, showed dozens of twinkling jewels of light. At least one building had some flood-lighting.

"Houses in Ashton appeared to specialise in fairy lights, several streets being made bright with strings of them on buildings.

"In Hotwells, a bonfire was built and a great crowd, scores of them standing on the no-longer-needed air raid shelters—stayed around it until well past midnight, singing to the strains of a piano accordion.

"There were other bonfires in the same vicinity, and at one the exuberant crowd dragged bunks from air-raid shelters to feed the flames.

"A piece of furniture which had been standing outside a second-hand shop elsewhere was whisked away to be used as fuel.

"Not far away, on a street corner, another big assembly made the night air ring with community singing, lustily rendered, and there was some dancing in the streets.

"In the nearby Trinity Church (damaged in an air raid) someone found a bell-rope and the clangour of a single bell echoed across the streets. Everywhere, in outskirts as well as city, lights blazed into the early hours. Bright flashes on the horizon also lit the sky well into the night. No one knew the cause—but for the first time since September 1939 everyone knew the origin was peaceful."

1946

THURSDAY MAY 30TH

"Detectives investigating the death of Mr R.N. Parrington Jackson, 32-year-old general manager of the Odeon Theatre, Bristol, found shot through the temples in his office last evening, have solved one mystery and are faced with two more.

"The mystery they have solved is the identity of the patron who phoned them from the cinema to report the shooting. This man has now come forward and has volunteered "a most helpful statement".

"The police are still trying, however, to find (1) the weapon and (2) a motive. Late this afternoon they reported "absolutely no new developments". They expected to be engaged at the Odeon all day today and possibly tomorrow.

"Mr Jackson's wife was at his bedside with police on hand when he died at Bristol Royal Infirmary at 3.35 a.m. today. It is understood he was unable to describe what had happened.

"Mr Jackson, who lived with his wife and four-year-old son at Zetland Road, was appointed manager of the Odeon in March 1940. He resumed his duties only seven weeks ago after $5\frac{1}{2}$ years in the Royal Navy.

"In true showmanlike fashion "the show went on" after Mr Jackson had been shot. But for a notice flashed on to the screen to appeal for a doctor, patrons watching a presentation of *The Light That Failed* had no inkling of the drama which was being enacted in another part of the building."

It was, and still is, one of Bristol's most sensational murders.

The film playing at the moment when the dashing, dinner-jacketed manager who had acted in the movies, driven across America by car in just five days and worked as a radio announcer was shot, was a thriller.

Six shots rang out. Five of them were on the soundtrack of *The Light That Failed*. The sixth was for real.

Forty-eight hours later, the police were no wiser, as the *Evening Post* revealed.

Friday's Post reported:

"While a watch was being maintained at Temple Meads and other West-country stations and at Avonmouth and other docks, police officers were taking statement after statement.

"All likely places, including blitzed ruins, have been combed for the weapon, but so far without result. There is strong reason to believe it was a .45 Service revolver.

"Police Have Two Theories.

"Several lines of inquiry are being pursued, following a day of methodical search, conferences, interviews and attempts to reconstruct the shooting, with officers impersonating Mr Jackson and his assailant.

"Police worked all night in the office where the shooting took place.

"Silhouetted against the curtains could occasionally be seen the figures of C.I.D. men who, with finger-print experts and photographers, were still scrutinising every inch of the room for possible clues.

"The possibility of suicide has been ruled out, leaving the theories of:

1—Mr Jackson returning to his office to surprise an intruder intent on robbery who shot his way out. It is known that Mr Jackson had taken the takings from the box-office to the safe in his private office. He then visited the operating box and was shot on returning to his office.

2—Mr Jackson being shot in a private quarrel with the intruder."

No money had been taken. The key to the safe was found in the dying man's pocket. The mystery remains unsolved.

1947

THURSDAY NOVEMBER 20TH

'Their' tune was 'People Will Say We're In Love' from the smash hit show *Oklahoma!*. Their faces were those of Britain's favourite and most photographed sweethearts and on November 20th, 1947 They married.

The Post's Royal Wedding Special was headlined simply: **The Whole World Wishes Her Happiness.**

And, of course, the Post had its staff up in London to get the Bristol angle on the event of the year.

"Five Bristolians, members of the 6th Navy Platoon, lined up in Whitehall, were right in the front row. They were PO E.J. Higgs, ABS Ogden, Hudson and Sweetman and Elec. Mech. Templar, all of them RNVR.

"All saw active service in the Navy during the war.

" 'I stared when I saw the Life Guards' PO Higgs told the Evening Post in London this afternoon.

" 'I couldn't have imagined anything so grand.

" 'But my biggest thrill was at the Retire. The Marine band formed up, the 6th Platoon fell in immediately behind and at the order, 'Royal Navy—Quick March!' we led the Naval contingent.

" 'The crowd gave us a shout that brought a lump into my throat.

" 'Before then we were standing at the 'present' and daren't stir a muscle. A kid at a window opposite was sucking a lemon watching us. She was laughing like anything.

" 'It seemed funny to her but it wasn't to us. Our throats were parched. We hadn't had a drink for four hours. But it was worth it.

" 'At a third storey window opposite us was Gracie Fields. After the return procession she burst out singing 'Sally', 'Now Is The Hour', 'Oh What A Wonderful Day'. She was singing her head off and the crowd joined in and gave her a big hand.

" 'Then there were Bob Hope, Robert Montgomery and Alexis Smith close by. Bob was doing his funny stuff. I could tell from the way everybody was laughing but I couldn't turn my head.

" 'And now I am off to buy the baby a present. Then I want to catch The Bristolian at 4.15 and tell the wife what a wonderful day it has been. She will want to know about the Princess's dress. I don't know much about dresses but Elizabeth looked beautiful, whatever she was wearing'.

"ABS Ogden is an old hand at Royal occasions. He was in the Diadem in the Vanguard escort on Their Majesty's South African trip, in the Rodney in '45 at Forsyth when the King inspected the Home Fleet and at Naval inspections by the King in Italy.

" 'But this beats all,' he said."

1948

SATURDAY JULY 3RD

It was the weekend that cricket-mad Bristol had longed for . . . the weekend the legendary Australian team came to town.

This was the first Test series English tour by the Down Under enemy since the end of the war. It was led by the mighty Don Bradman and the visit to play Gloucestershire at the County Ground in Bishopston had the whole of the West Country agog.

The Tests themselves were blow-by-blow front page news in the Post with each day's Page One lead story written by our very own celebrity Test correspondent, one Wally Hammond.

The Bristol clash was no more than a practice for Bradman's mighty Aussies, but that didn't stop excitement reaching fever pitch.

Even the news, announced on Friday July 2nd, that Bradman himself would be resting and not taking part in the match couldn't dampen the enthusiasm.

The Post warned that afternoon that "Bristol Tramways are advising people to board buses at the Centre and not to try to pick them up en route". Extra staff and seating were arranged for the County Ground.

The following day the Post ran special editions to commemorate the great event.

"The news that the Australians had won the toss and would bat spread like wildfire. Hundreds were still pouring in when Australia's captain Lindsay Hassett and Basil Allen went out to inspect the wicket.

"Then the crowd, estimated at 18,000, settled down to enjoy a spate of run-getting on a thoroughly easy wicket.

"Morris, in enterprising mood, took heavy toll of the bowling after Hassett, who led the Australians in place of Bradman, won the toss.

"Cook, however, struck the first blow for Gloucestershire, getting Barnes brilliantly caught in the slips by Crapp.

"The Tetbury left-hander was again cheered when he lured Hassett out of his crease and Andy Wilson whipped off his bails in a trice."

But any dream of Boys Own heroics against the mighty Bradman side were rapidly dispelled—and the crowds who had poured up the Gloucester Road loved every moment of it.

Monday's Post carried a composite picture made up from individual pictures across its centre pages which gave a 300 degree view of the gigantic crowd jammed into every available space at the County Ground.

The Aussies went on to score 774 for seven "their highest in the tour so far" our local cricket correspondent John Coe reported.

The greatest Gloucestershire honours went to local hero Jack Crapp. He was not out for 100, but it couldn't stop Australia winning by an innings and 363 runs.

Wally Hammond watched . . . and approved, suggesting that the local lad might find a niche in the England side for the next Test.

"'I would say it is no certainty that Edrich will play. He may well give way to Crapp.'" Edrich did play, and so did Crapp. And Bristol enjoyed one of its most spectacular weekends of international cricket.

1949

SEPTEMBER

The Brab put the pride back into post-war Bristol and the maiden flight of the giant airliner, then the biggest aircraft in the world, was an international event reported by newspapers and newsreels across the world.

The Brabazon, Britain's bid to re-establish its lead as a top plane maker on the lucrative international routes, was a beauty. She was slim, elegant and looked exactly like the classy lady she was meant to be . . . a rich man and woman's magic transport to glamorous destinations. Her specifications included a double-decker interior with private First Class cabins, a 32-seat cinema, a swish cocktail bar and a luxurious lounge.

The silver prototype made its first flight at Filton on Sunday September 5th, 1949 and the Post joined in the fun, reporting Bristol Aeroplane Company joint managing director Reginald Verdon-Smith's delighted comment to test pilot Captain Bill Pegg: 'A splendid run! Well done!' Lord Brabazon, the plane's namesake, commented: 'My faith has been justified. I have never seen any trial go off so smoothly'.

The brief flight meant a leisurely aerial stroll over north Bristol, Chipping Sodbury

Christened as "the biggest landplane in the world", the Brabazon was designed to carry over 100 passengers in luxury to New York.

and then Avonmouth before the return to Filton.

The Queen, later to become the Queen Mum, paid a visit to Filton with her young daughter Princess Margaret shortly afterwards. The Post was there to record the Royal inspection of Bristol's best.

"The Queen and Princess Margaret, on a surprise informal visit today, spent 15 minutes inside the Brabazon and were shown how to handle the controls by Captain Bill Pegg.

"They were obviously thrilled by their experiences, so much so that they squeezed their way into the wings behind the powerful engines. The Royal visitors were also greatly impressed by the mammoth hangar which houses the Brabazon. The Queen likened it to the Crystal Palace.

"Mr Pegg found both the Queen and the Princess intensely interested in the actual operation of the plane.

"As the Royal party had approached the Brabazon's 117 ft high hangar, the Queen and the Princess said they were 'staggered' by its enormous size and pleased with the colour scheme and spacious windows.

"Princess Margaret blinked as she looked up into the vast spaciousness of the hangar.

"Speaking to Mr L.D. Atkinson, chief engineer of the Brabazon, the Queen said: 'It must have been a thrill flying in the aircraft for the first time'. He agreed and the Queen added, 'It is a very nice aeroplane.'"

Nice the Brab certainly was. She droned her way around the West Country and along the South Coast and pleased the crowds who watched her stately progress. But she was hopelessly slow and jet airliners lay just around the corner. Three years later with just one Brab built and a second only half completed, the project was cancelled.

The Post's final verdict? A wistful editorial which sighed: "And so farewell to the great Might-Have-Been."

1950

JULY

The 1950s came in like a breath of fresh air. A new decade, new resolutions, new hopes after the war-scarred Forties.

Plans for the following year's futuristic Festival of Britain on London's South Bank were setting the pace for a country fed up to the back teeth with the rationing, shortages and make-and-mend years of post-war austerity.

We'd won the war five years before and in Bristol, like the rest of the country, people had had enough of the sight of damaged or unpainted buildings, a tatty city centre and an overall dowdiness.

The Fifties had arrived and it was time to get Bristol and Britain moving again.

And it looked as if things were happening at last. There were firm plans to create a new space-age shopping centre in Broadmead. Above all there was the prospect of a new Council House befitting a city as famous as Bristol.

This was Bristol's biggest, boldest development with a magnificently imposing building taking shape alongside one of the city centre's grandest open spaces, College Green. It was to replace the old Council House on the corner of Broad Street and Corn Street, for years far too small for such a large city and growing city bureaucracy.

Work on the grandiose, crescent-shaped headquarters began in the 1930s but the project had to be mothballed for the six years of the war. Now it was a-building again, and Bristol wanted a perfect setting for its new architectural gem.

College Green as it was in 1950 wouldn't do, said Bristol's leaders on July 26th when they announced that they planned to spend £10,000 lowering the level of the green to give future generations of Bristolians a civic centre to be proud of. The suggestion caused an outcry from some quarters who campaigned to Save Old College Green.

The Post reported:

"Alderman Frank Sheppard, chairman of the Municipal Buildings Committee, said College Green was the property of the Dean and Chapter of the Cathedral who were "delighted" at the proposal to restore the Green to its original level. It would present a much better vista from the Cathedral.

"The whole question of the new Council House was raised as long ago as 1929 when expert architects were appointed to go into the proposals and the Council agreed in 1938 to the lowering.

"The Green was originally at the same level as the Cathedral and had only been raised after some rubbish from works near the river had been dumped there.

" 'It is not a case of vandalism of ancient ground, as has been suggested by some people; we are only putting the Green into its original position'.

"He would not comment on whether the committee intended going ahead with the bulldozing work immediately or "holding its hand" and preparing another report for the Council in view of the "shower of protest"."

Within a year came approval for the lay-out of the lowered College Green complete with a pool to front the Council House and broad paths across the Green.

The lowering of College Green in progress.

1951

SUNDAY APRIL 22ND

The Gloucestershire Regiment became the Glorious Glosters in the battle which began that night . . . the Battle of the Imjin River.

The confrontation involved courage and tenacity of such an extraordinary nature that the American troops nearby could hardly believe the epic that was unfolding before their eyes.

Just 600 men from Gloucestershire and Bristol took on an attacking force of 25,000—and held them at bay for four days. It was a turning point in the Korean War.

"The magnificent battle fought by the 1st Bn. Gloucestershire Regiment against the Chinese Communists on the south bank of the Imjin River was probably the most epic and gallant fought in this war.

"It was a determined stand against overwhelming odds which undoubtedly took the sting out of the enemy's initial thrusts against the United Nations forces.

"Early on the night of April 22nd, the Glosters, dug in on positions on a hill overlooking the bend in the river, made first contact with enemy forces.

"A patrol of the Glosters was sent down to the ferry but, after making contact, was forced to withdraw through the battalion lines owing to heavy crossfire.

"Tightening their defences, the battalion, after a night being machine-gunned from all angles, was attacked in great strength on St George's Day by hundreds of fanatical Chinese troops, tearing up the hillside with cover fire from all surrounding hills for their advance.

"From then on, the battalion was constantly under enemy fire.

"A company on the left flank was soon overrun and B company was forced to withdraw into other defensive positions but D company was ordered to hold its forward positions with only the minimum supply of ammunition, no food or water.

"This remaining company with the battalion command post, machine gun platoon and mortar platoon, held out against terrible odds in a position completely exposed to enemy fire and where no help could be given.

"The commanding officer, Lt. Col. J.P. Carne, who has been highly praised by the few men of the regiment who fought their way back to the Brigade areas, was in continual radio contact with Brigade until the wireless batteries failed.

"Only when the situation became more desperate and casualties mounted did he give the order for the small force left to withdraw, remaining behind himself to assist the medical officer with the wounded.

"Many attempts were made by British and American tanks to relieve the hard-pressed Glosters, but the difficult ground and narrow roads made their task impossible.

"An airdrop was requested but it was unable to supply the besieged troops on account of enemy positions.

"The only meagre supply made to the unit during the four days' encirclement was made by one of the Glosters' officers who dropped Bren guns and ammunition wrapped in blankets from an American scout plane."

Fred Carne, as he was affectionately known, was awarded the VC. Veterans of the Imjin won not only the right to wear the Battle Honour Imjin but also the United States presidential citation on their sleeve.

Carne and his men were captured and endured two brutal years as POWs. Their return to the West Country in the autumn of 1953 almost overshadowed the Coronation as Bristol and Gloucestershire saluted its heroes.

Wenvoe Triumphs: Reception "Almost Perfect"

RAIN-DRENCHED CEREMONY

CRACKLING thunder and vicious lightning over both South Wales and the Bristol area could not mar the opening ceremony of the world's most powerful television transmitter at Wenvoe. Reception throughout the West was almost perfect, writes Peter Woon.

When the new station began its first programme viewers could see the black clouds hovering overhead. And as Earl De La Warr, the Postmaster - General, made his official opening speech the rain came down in torrents.

But the ceremony went through, and the Earl, getting slowly drenched as he stood in the open without a macintosh, finished his piece and pulled aside the flag of the B.B.C. and the Union Jack, to reveal the Corporation's coat-of-arms.

And so the West—and Wales—was officially received into the national television network.

First of the "distinguished company" of over 300 gathered at Wenvoe to be introduced to the viewers by commentator Wynford Vaughan Thomas was Alderman Percy Cann, Deputy Lord Mayor of Bristol.

Then the two cameras at the station panned around the rest of the crowd.

INTO THE CROWD

And those in the West who were seeing television for the first time —as several thousands of them were—could then gain some idea of its potentialities.

Into the crowd went the cameras to pick out individuals and bring them into the viewers' homes. There was the lady in a flowered hat who smiled, laughed and then gaily waved her hand. There was the self-conscious gentleman with glasses. There was another who abandoned all restraint and roared with laughter. This among a "distinguished company."

Before the opening, the narrow confines of the new station approach were filled by the Morriston Orpheus Male Choir, the Brynmawr Dancers and—from Winchester—the Band of the 1st Bn. King's Royal Rifles, the "Greenjackets."

"HAPPY VIEWING"

For the remainder of the evening the national television network devoted itself to programmes which emphasised—and welcomed —the entry of a potential four-and-a-half-million new viewers into the national fold.

Announcer Sylvia Peters and Mary Malcolm had donned the new dresses they had chosen at a special fashion show earlier in the week, and both made neat little speeches wishing a "specially good evening and many happy hours of viewing to you in the West and Wales."

In two hours viewers saw pictures taken in places from Washington to Greenland; and, at the same time, a good slice of that two hours was devoted to publicising some of the virtues and talents of the West itself.

A group of Yugoslav officers will attend the British Army's autumn manoeuvres in the British zone of Germany later this month.

Separate Stations Call

CHANNEL A FRONTIER?

LADY Megan Lloyd George greeting Wenvoe on behalf of the Welsh people before the T V cameras last night, said she could do so only with "muted enthusiasm."

For what they really wanted, she said, was "our own earth and all that therein is."

There could be no true "marriage" between the West and Welsh regions, and, while there was "great sympathy" between the two, there was also a wide difference of interests and way of life.

"The Bristol Channel is a frontier between two countries," she said.

There had once been a radio tie-up between the two regions and she thought all would agree it had not been "a crashing success."

"WE SHALL FIGHT"

One of the fundamental differences existing was that of languages. "Welsh is a national treasure house — we are going to fight for it."

So, welcoming the opening of the new station "a little nervously," she added: "I hope we will not rest until each region has a separate station of its own; let us unite to separate."

WESTON STORM
Twelve Hours' Thunder

Weston-super-Mare had 12 hours of thunder and lightning from mid-day yesterday—but the town has completely escaped damage.

At 2 a.m. today lightning was still flashing and thunder rumbling, but Weston firemen, constantly at the alert for emergency pumping-out calls, were not summoned.

This morning only slight rain was falling and the sky was much clearer; yesterday afternoon buses, cars, and coaches travelled with headlights on.

TESTS IMPRESS

Bristol Civil Defence officials are "extremely pleased" with the result of the tests conducted during the week of their latest walkie-talkie apparatus. Both the short-distance and the long-range tests from Dundry, the the Cabot Tower, and the Observatory proved satisfactory.

Between 4,000 and 5,000 leaflets giving details of the general reconnaissance group of the C.D. Corps, for which 200 recruits are required, were handed out. The apparatus will be used in the large exercises during the big recruiting drive in October.

SYLVIA PETERS making the first announcement.

THE POSTMASTER-GENERAL opening the transmitter.

A WEST-COUNTRY excerpt from "Serenade."

LOUIS KENTNER at the piano.

RADIO CAR CATCH
Five Minutes' Notice

Five minutes after a Bristol police car had been informed by wireless of a Jaguar missing from a city car park, the car was seen, chased, and stopped as it was heading for Gloucester.

"This is a remarkable instance of how wireless has revolutionised the catching of thieves," said prosecuting solicitor, Mr. W. J. Hutchinson, at Bristol today.

Edward Anthony Baker (26), of Frobisher Hall, near Stone, Staffs, was fined £20 for taking and driving away the car from Wine St. car park, £10 for driving without insurance, and £1 for driving without a licence.

He was said to have used his knowledge as an electrical engineer to start the car's engine without an ignition key.

93 CLASSES
Bristol Firm's Show

1952

FRIDAY AUGUST 15TH

The Post was packed with ads for television sets . . . "The superb Cossor . . . 64 guineas, tax paid".

And for other essential equipment . . . "The Aerialite Aeradoor at 32s . . . attach to the skirting board" or the rooftop "Aerialite Aeraitch" aerial with its then novel H shape, at £7 19s.

It was the day the 'goggle box' came to Bristol with the opening of the Wenvoe transmitter to beam programmes to an estimated 20,000 viewers in the West. "One family in 25 in Bristol now own a TV set" the Post said.

The next day the paper reported:

"Crackling thunder and vicious lightning over both South Wales and Bristol could not mar the opening ceremony of the world's most powerful TV transmitter at Wenvoe. Reception throughout the West was almost perfect.

"When the new station began its first programme, viewers could see the black clouds hovering overhead, and as Earl De La Warr, the Postmaster General, made his official speech, the rain came down in torrents.

"But the ceremony went through and the Earl, getting thoroughly drenched in his suit in the open without a mackintosh, finished his piece and pulled aside the flag of the BBC and the Union Jack to reveal a Corporation coat of arms.

"First of the 'distinguished company' of over 300 gathered at Wenvoe to be introduced to the viewers by commentator Wynford Vaughan Thomas was Ald.

Percy Cann, Deputy Lord Mayor of Bristol.

"Then the two cameras at the station panned around the rest of the crowd and those in the West homes who were seeing TV for the first time, as several thousand of them were, were given some idea of its potentialities.

"Into the crowd went the cameras to pick out individuals and bring them into the viewers' homes.

"There was the lady in the flowered hat who smiled, laughed and then quickly waved her hand. There was the self-conscious gentleman who wore glasses. There was another who abandoned all restraint and roared with laughter.

"Announcers Sylvia Peters and Mary Malcolm had donned the new dresses they had chosen at a special fashion show earlier in the week and both made neat little speeches wishing a 'specially good evening and many happy hours of viewing to you in the West and Wales'.

"In two hours viewers saw pictures taken in places from Washington to Greenland and at the same time a good proportion of that two hours was devoted to publicising some of the virtues and talents of the West itself".

The Post chose that day to announce its latest 'scoop'.

TV's favourite puppet, Muffin The Mule, was to have his very own comic strip—starting in your favourite evening paper on Monday!

1953

TUESDAY JUNE 2ND

The New Elizabethan Age was beginning . . . and Bristol celebrated its arrival in style.

For weeks the forthcoming Coronation of the young Queen Elizabeth had captured everyone's imagination as the most exciting national celebration since the Festival of Britain two years before.

And when Coronation Day came at last, Bristol made sure that it was truly memorable with street parties, sports and dancing on the Downs, firework displays, a river pageant on the City Docks and city-wide Coronation illuminations.

The real fun was on the streets of Bristol and in London. Tens of thousands of Bristolians made the pilgrimage to the capital by car, coach and train.

Pat Price was the Post's girl among the rain-soaked crowds in central London, tracking down local folk who were up for the Coronation Day spectacular.

She reported:

"One young man told me: 'This is something like the old spirit that brought us together at a less happy time. If for that alone, the Coronation has done a great job.'

"They were a happy, good-natured crowd who rigged home-made canopies and tents between the steel crush bars and shop-window hoardings.

"They shared not only their blankets but their sandwiches, the soup they had brought in Thermos flasks, the magazines, the jokes and news of things they talk about back home.

"Miss Gladys Scott of Berrydale Avenue, Bridgwater put straw into her shoes and made a pillow from newspapers for a 12-year-old schoolgirl. 'I've promised to look after her because her mother, a nurse, was on duty all night at hospital.'

"Miss Deborah Wright (19) of Clifton Park Road, Clifton was dressed in a tracksuit like her fellow students of Bedford College of Physical Education. During their wait a passing motorist had handed them a flask of rum—'to keep out the cold, dears'—and they did folk dancing during the night".

Another Post reporter, Peter Woon travelled by coach:

"Like the pussy cat, we went to London to see the Queen. There were a thousand of us when we left Bristol in our handsome motor-coaches.

"At the back was our oldest hand in Coronation-going, Miss L. Brock, fruit shop manageress of Kingston Buildings, Kingsdown. Her clothes were festooned (there was no other word for it) with red, white and blue ribbon and she understandably looked more than a little proud as she told us:

"'I went up to London for the Coronation in 1937. Got a wonderful view in Oxford Street. Some people say it's a waste of time to travel all this way for a glimpse of things, but they don't know what it's like. I wouldn't have missed the Coronation for the world.'

"Next to Miss Brock sat Mrs V.M. Stowell, a cheerful, grey-haired widow of Hampton Park, Redland. On her head was her own crowning masterpiece of red velvet on the back of which was a simple little brooch of the Queen. Another brooch was on her lapel and both ornaments were beribboned.

"Said Mrs Stowell: 'This hat was made from the remnants of a frock I wore at the Coronation ball in Bristol in 1937'.

"Yes, we were a mixed bunch, our jobs different, our clothes different and we had never met before.

"But today we were united in our destination and, more, in our thoughts."

1954

FEBRUARY

It must have been the most expensive bellyflop in the history of Bristol's aviation industry, the day the second prototype of the Britannia airliner landed ignominiously in the Severnside mud.

She was to become famous and well-loved as the Whispering Giant and a workhorse of some of the world's great air routes.

But the day that faults in the test plane's engines forced famous test pilot Bill Pegg to dump Britannia in the Gloucestershire mud, sealed Britannia's fate. She would never make the first division in the league table of successful civil airliners.

"The Britannia, on a routine flight, was crash-landed by BAC's chief test pilot Mr Bill Pegg with one of the engines on fire after he had searched the area in the hope of finding a suitable landing strip.

"One fuel tank exploded as the plane came down, but the resulting fire was quickly extinguished and the fire appliances sent to the scene from a wide area were needed only for standby purposes.

"Mr R.A. Bright, a clerk at the Aust-Beachley ferry, told the Evening Post how the plane pancaked into the mud at Littleton, about a mile and a quarter from the ferry.

"'We watched it through binoculars. As the plane landed there was a small explosion. There was a small fire which was promptly extinguished.

"'We watched the crew clamber out. All of them seemed to be unhurt. We immediately rang Filton with the message that the plane had crashed'.

"After seeing that his crew were safe and that everything was being done to secure his aircraft, Mr Pegg himself drove a BAC staff car back to Filton.

"Mrs E.M. Nott, licensee's wife of the White Hart Inn, which is only half a mile away from the scene of the crash, told the Evening Post that the plane had come to rest on the banks of the Severn near the Littleton brickworks.

"Mr M. Charles, a foreman brickworker, who, with others, ran to the scene, said that everyone was amazingly calm.

"Before they could reach the plane, they had 150 yards of mud to negotiate.

"While efforts were being made to secure the Britannia this afternoon, BAC technicians were going aboard to remove valuable instruments and equipment.

"The first hint that Britannia was in trouble was a short radio message from Mr Pegg.

"A second message said: 'Going to try to land at Filton'.

"Then came the third and last message to Filton control tower; 'Going to crash land at Littleton'.

"When the engine trouble developed, he steered and coaxed the machine over the only possible place where it could land without extensive damage—mud on the Severn.

"Gradually he brought her down parallel to the shore line. The machine landed on its belly, just missing a line of posts which would have ripped it open.

"It skidded for more than 200 yards across the mud, shedding an engine on its way and churning up sprays of mud and water like a snow plough before it came to rest facing the ebbing tide."

The mishap scuppered the Britannia. It caused long delays in her development and by the time she did go into service the Boeing 707 jet airliner would be available within a couple of years, and the world's airlines knew it.

A super plane, a triumph of Bristol aviation skill but a plane too late in a changing world . . . thanks to that muddy baptism.

1955

WEDNESDAY JUNE 22ND

One chapter in the history of Bristol aviation came to its close . . . another started.

On June 22nd 1955 the Post reported triumphantly that "after 10 years of negotiation Bristol Corporation has been offered Lulsgate airport for sale or lease by the Minister of Transport".

Readers were told that it would cost £55,000 to buy the derelict wartime air station with its 335 acres of land just off the A38 near Bristol. It was estimated that it would cost £42,794 a year to run the airport and that income would be £6,500 a year for the time being.

It spelt the death-knell for the 500-acre civic airport which had been opened two years before the Post began, in 1930, by Prince George, Duke of York (later King George VI) at Whitchurch.

Whitchurch's greatest moments of glory had come during the war when, in 1941, a daily service was begun to Lisbon, capital of neutral Portugal. It made little Whitchurch the only civil air gateway from Britain to the Americas, Africa and the Far East.

"The airport was daily thronged with VIPs helping the war effort. Royalty, heads of governments, ambassadors, stage and film stars and officers of all ranks of all services were daily coming and going."

Imperial Airways and British Airways had even moved their fleets to Whitchurch for the war.

But Whitchurch, within the city boundary, couldn't be developed further as the town grew around it and post-war Bristol argued over whether to turn the existing Filton airfield into the civic aerodrome or to develop Lulsgate, a few miles south of the city.

Bristol wanted to turn itself into an international air centre and in April 1954, Mr John Profumo, Parliamentary Secretary to the Ministry of Transport and Civil Aviation confirmed that "he is prepared to lease Lulsgate Aerodrome to the Corporation for development as their airport".

Bristol also wanted Lulsgate to be sponsored by the Government or at least given some financial help. Nothing doing.

" 'There is no question of the Government taking over and running Lulsgate or any other West of England airfield as an international airport,' " Mr Boyd Carpenter, the transport minister, told the Post.

So Bristol went ahead with Lulsgate by itself. On September 13th, 1955 the Post reported that "Ald. V.J. Ross, chairman of the Airport Committee, told the City Council: 'I hope we shall be able to operate Lulsgate in June of next year.' "

He didn't make his deadline. Lulsgate was officially opened on May 1st, 1957 by the Duchess of Kent who emphasised that the new airport would establish "Bristol's place as one of the country's leading air centres."

1956

WEDNESDAY JUNE 27TH

The re-opening of a restored bar in St Nicholas Market in the heart of old Bristol hardly looked like a moment of British post-war history. But it was.

No-one afterwards could blame the Post's man sent to cover the story of Night One in the refurbished bar at the ancient Rummer tavern which had been taken over by the Bristol company Hort's, which was run by Frank and Aldo Berni and Paul Rosse.

How was he to know that he was witnessing the opening salvo in a revolution that was to change the eating out habits of the British for the next two decades? But he was. He was among the first to hear news of a 'Berni', as a meal at one of the scores of Berni restaurants up and down the country would soon be known.

The company was named after Hort's restaurant which the Berni brothers had bought in 1943. After the ending of meat rationing in 1954, the Bernis hoped to import American-style, controlled portion steak and chips catering, served in as authentic an Olde English atmosphere as possible.

The Rummer, sometimes claimed as one of the oldest inns in the country, was to be their prototype. They heard that the Bristol Corporation-owned pub was available and moved quickly. They won the tenancy and called in a designer who exploited all the period details. The place was a rabbit warren and it perfectly suited their plans for a series of bars and restaurants . . . and steak grill rooms.

Opening night on June 27th, 1956 brought plenty of interest.

"In three short weeks a complete transformation has been effected. Thirteen coats of old paint, nearly half an inch thick, had to be removed before the redecoration could begin.

"As customers moved into the new bar, work on dismantling the old one began. Some of the pipes bringing beer from the cellar have been found to be at least 100 years old.

"Looking through the window on to the Market, one's eyes are caught by a notice recalling the presence of Morrison's old restaurant. 'Lunches at 1s 6d and 1s 9d.'

"These prices, I am told, prevailed until just before the war—an unpleasant reminder of the tremendous rise in the cost of catering and the difficulties now facing all restaurateurs.

"When the ground floor is finished the new occupiers hope to open a grill room on the first floor, but that will be some time in the future".

The grill room with its soon-to-be-famous limited menu was open within months. Any difficulties facing the Berni restaurant were over weeks after that. The Berni revolution had begun.

1957

WEDNESDAY MAY 29TH

Bristol had watched the two giants take shape alongside each other on the Horsefair . . . the two swish department stores that would put Bristol back on the map as the region's top shopping centre.

There was the "ocean liner-shaped" Lewis's complete with its exciting plans for a roof garden overlooking central Bristol and its huge neighbour Jones.

Four years earlier Bristol had been agog when the Post revealed on October 2nd, 1953 that:

"Work will begin soon on Bristol's largest departmental store.

"Today Jones and Co Ltd, who lost their store in Wine St and High St in the blitz of November 1940, released details of the proposed new building.

"It will rise to five floors. It will extend over the area bounded by Bond St and St James's Barton on one side and Milk St (later to be called Horsefair)—on the other.

"Its total area will be 210,000 square feet. It will cost £1 million.

"So Jones's will have the biggest store in the city again—their pre-1940 one was the largest in the West. And standing beside their new building will be another giant, Lewis's. Work, it is hoped, will begin before Christmas and be complete in two years."

It took longer than that but the public didn't really mind. Now, at last, Bristol was making an effort to re-establish itself as the shopping centre of the West.

The Post carried regular reports as the two huge buildings rose and rose.

By May 16th 1957, everyone was excited.

"The first of the two giant stores being built in The Horsefair—that of Jones and Co—opens a fortnight today.

"Nearly 300 workers are now engaged on the big task of getting the store—which covers a bigger area than any other in the West Country—ready on time.

"The opening marks a triumph for all those concerned with the project. It was intended when work was started three years ago that the store should be ready by May 8th, but since then 'many, many difficulties' have been experienced with the supply of materials and labour.

"A staff of 750 has been recruited, the greater proportion of them from Bristol.

"Since Jones and Co. lost its old headquarters in High Street it has carried on in eight small premises in various parts of the city. All these are being closed with the exception of the one in Regent Street, Kingswood".

The store opened in style on May 29th with a celebratory dinner at 8 p.m.

Guests worked their way through a menu which read, the Post reported:

Melon Cocktail
Lobster Newburg

Roast Fillet of Beef "Bristol" with noisette potatoes, new potatoes, French beans, garden peas, green salad and endive salad.

Jones' Progress or Souffle En Surprise

Various Cheeses and Biscuits

Fruit Baskets
Coffee
Petit Fours

Lewis's took a little longer to arrive. It opened on September 26th that year. Broadmead, Bristol's new shopping centre, was well under way.

LEWIS'S
In The Haymarket, Bristol

The building of a super-store

● NOW a Bristol landmark, the new store stands majestically against a dramatic sky. But there were many stages to go through before this result was reached. Below we picture some of them, and in this supplement more pictures help tell the story of the building.

● Bare trees and a barren look mark the site as it is first fenced off. Soon it is transformed into a gigantic hole (right) for the foundations and lower floors of the new building.

● Gradually as steelwork and stone facing goes up the store takes shape. At last it is opening day and shoppers pour in.

1958

FRIDAY DECEMBER 5TH

Grace was the electronic robot, gracious was the Queen that afternoon . . . and dialling a phone number was never quite the same again.

It was the day Her Majesty came to Bristol with the Duke of Edinburgh to inaugurate the latest marvel of the Young Elizabethan age, direct telephone dialling to other parts of the country.

Bristol was chosen for the first-ever S.T.D. exchange and the Monarch was invited to do the honours of dialling the nation's first-ever S.T.D. phone call.

The Post ran a Royal edition that day:

"The Queen in Bristol this afternoon made the country's first twopenny trunk call, thus opening a new telephone service for 18,000 homes on the Bristol Central Exchange.

"Standing on a dais at the exchange, the Queen dialled 031 CAL 3636. And 365 miles away, the Lord Provost of Edinburgh picked up the phone to receive her call.

"The Queen made her call, at the invitation of the Postmaster-General Mr Ernest Marples on a streamlined, light blue telephone connected directly to Grace, the electronic robot which controls S.T.D. only a few feet behind her.

"As she dialled, each numeral and letter of the Lord Provost's number flashed up on a special indicator at the back of the dais. The 150 specially invited guests in the first floor room at the exchange where Grace is housed could watch each stage as her call went through.

"She said: 'This is the Queen speaking from Bristol. Good afternoon, Lord Provost'.

"The Lord Provost replied: 'Good afternoon, your Majesty. May I with humble duty offer you the loyal greetings of the City of Edinburgh'.

"The Queen then said: 'Would you please convey my greetings to them. I am always interested in any development that brings my people closer together. In a few moments Bristol subscribers will be able to make trunk calls, by merely dialling the right number in a radius of 300 miles. In time, the whole United Kingdom will enjoy the advantage of this new service that the Post Office has introduced'.

"The Lord Provost concluded: 'May I express my gratitude to your Majesty for the honour that you have done to me and to Scotland by making the first call in this service to me'.

"One of the most interested spectators was the Duke of Edinburgh who had earlier accompanied the Queen on a tour of the exchange and of the Twopenny Telephone exhibition in the Equity and Law Building in Baldwin Street.

"In the exhibition Mr Marples, a lively little figure full of enthusiasm, had demonstrated to the Queen the advantage to her when, eventually, Windsor Castle is connected to London by S.T.D.

"Then he told the Queen she will be able to dial Buckingham Palace direct from Windsor Castle without having to enlist the aid of an operator. It will be at least 1960 before this happens.

"On the special stand which has been set up to make demonstrations of S.T.D. possible, he invited the Queen to make a trial call before going to the exchange for the real thing.

"After the Queen had made the call, the Postmaster-General presented to the Queen the instrument with which she had made it."

The Queen made the first call on the revolutionary S.T.D. service from Bristol Central Telephone Exchange.

1959

THURSDAY OCTOBER 1ST

The Brabazon in the 40s . . . the Britannia in the 50s . . . so what new model would Bristol's planemakers come up with for the 1960s to tackle the new overwhelming commercial superiority of their American rivals?

Planes were big, big news in the 1950s and this was the heyday of the Air Correspondent.

Developing new aircraft was risky, both financially and physically. The Brab had proved a financial flop and Britannia had suffered two crashes before she became a modest success.

The test pilots who tried out the new models were heroes of their day and the dangers of pioneering had been there for all to see; first in the battering taken by the little jets which at last cracked the sound barrier, and then by the horrors of metal fatigue, revealed when Comet pioneered the jetliner age with tragic consequences.

So where would Bristol go after Britannia? The answer came in an *Evening Post* scoop which confirmed rumours that had been circulating both at Filton and in political circles.

"Bristol Aircraft Ltd have produced startling designs for two new aircraft – one a revolutionary supersonic airliner and the other a slow, cheap-to-run ferry aircraft.

"No details of the supersonic project have been released by the company but the Post can reveal that it is known as the Type 198 and that top men in the British aircraft industry recently met at Filton to discuss its potential.

"The design of the Type 198 arises from the report of the Supersonic Transport Aircraft Committee set up by the Government in 1956. They recommended the building of a 150-seat 1,350 miles per hour aircraft and a 100-seater 810 miles per hour aircraft of shorter range.

"A few weeks ago it became known that Bristol Aircraft Ltd and the Hawker Siddeley group might become contenders on a joint approach for the supersonic project.

"The magnitude of the task—development costs would be about £150 million—means that it would have to be a combined effort with probably most of our aircraft companies participating."

The Anglo-French Concorde agreement would come later. But the Concorde project, which went on to cost a real figure of £1,000 million in its development, had found its home in Bristol.

49

1960

MONDAY APRIL 17TH

The death of a rock and roll legend on the local scene didn't even make page one of the *Evening Post* on April 17th, 1960.

Whoever was in charge of choosing that day's main stories for the Post had never heard of 'Summertime Blues', 'C'mon Everybody' or 'Three Steps To Heaven'.

And the name Eddie Cochran clearly rang no bells at all when the morning news conference was called.

Although one of the most influential figures in late 50s teen culture and later a hero of the great hall of fame of young, dead rockers like Buddy Holly, Jimi Hendrix, Jim Morrison, Otis Redding and John Lennon had died in a tragic road crash on the Post's 'patch', the event was only given sparse coverage.

Turn to Page One that Monday and you'll search in vain for the tale of Cochran's death. You have to turn the pages to find the news, and even then Eddie Cochran's demise isn't the introduction.

"Two American recording stars, Eddie Cochran and Gene Vincent, who headed the bill in a rock'n'roll show at Bristol Hippodrome last week, and were due to fly home to America, were involved in a crash yesterday.

"Mr Cochran died, without regaining consciousness, at St Martin's Hospital, Bath yesterday afternoon. Mr Vincent, with a fractured collarbone, is still detained there.

"Within an hour of leaving Bristol for London after the last performance on Saturday, the hire car in which they were travelling collided with a lamp standard at Rowden Hill on the outskirts of Chippenham.

"Mr Cochran's body will eventually be taken back to America for burial.

"There were two other passengers, Miss Sharon Sheeley (20), an American songwriter and Mr Patrick Tompkins (29), a theatrical agent of St James Road, Camberwell, London.

"They too are detained at St Martin's Hospital, Miss Sheeley with injuries to back and thigh, and Mr Tomkins with facial injuries and a suspected fracture of the base of the skull.

"Neither Mr Vincent nor his two friends were said last night to be on the danger list.

"The driver of the car, Mr George Martin of Bristol, was unhurt.

"There were no other vehicles involved. Mr Tompkins said: 'Just outside Chippenham the front tyre blew out and we skidded sideways into a lamp standard'.

"He added that he had been planning to take a train back to London from Bristol but Mr Vincent suggested travelling by taxi."

The Everly brothers, Don and Phil, were in Bristol the next day and were deeply shocked by the news. They rang the Bath hospital to ask if Sharon Sheeley could receive visitors and later came to her bedside to comfort the gifted, sparky young songwriter who lay injured and devastated by the tragedy. She recovered and returned home.

The taxi driver was later fined and disqualified for dangerous driving.

As for Eddie Cochran, his reputation as rock'n'roll's equivalent of James Dean grew and grew.

His small collection of songs are now regarded as some of the classics of early rock'n'roll.

1961

MONDAY MAY 8TH

Lord Stansgate brought Westminster to a halt that day . . . the day that the self-styled Anthony Wedgwood Benn arrived at the House of Commons to claim the Parliamentary seat he'd just won in Bristol.

He had first won it as Mr Wedgwood Benn a decade earlier, after Bristol South-East Labour party adopted him as its Parliamentary candidate. He was just 25.

But there was a time bomb ticking away throughout his 10 years as one of the youngest MPs in the land. Benn's father was a peer, Lord Stansgate, and Benn would inherit the title when he died. And that meant, by the rules of the day, that when plain Benn became Lord Stansgate, he must leave the House of Commons and take his rightful place in the House of Lords.

The Bristol MP, with hefty allies from both sides of the political divide, campaigned to give peers the right to renounce their titles. Attempt after attempt failed.

And then, in November 1960, his father collapsed and died of a heart attack in the House of Lords and Anthony Wedgwood Benn became automatically barred from taking his place in the Commons.

That didn't stop him fighting the by-election which followed his elevation to the peerage and it didn't stop a dramatic increase in his support. He doubled his majority to more than 13,000.

There was trouble to follow.

On May 8th, 1961 he arrived at Westminster to claim his place in the House of Commons. Everyone held their breath to see what would happen.

The Post's political editor John Guinery was there to watch the fun:

"Mr Anthony Wedgwood Benn was barred from entering the House of Commons this afternoon on the instruc-tions of the Speaker, Sir Harry Hylton-Foster, when he turned up in the wake of his Bristol South-East by-election victory.

Anthony Wedgwood Benn pictured with his wife Caroline.

"Shortly after the Speaker had taken the chair in the Chamber, Mr Benn went up to the door flanked by his two sponsors, Mr Herbert Bowden, the Labour chief whip, and Mr W.A. Wilkins, MP for Bristol South.

"About 20 supporters cheered him at the St Stephen's entrance. He held up his certificate of election which, he said, would enable him to take his seat.

"Mr Bowden later described what happened: 'Mr Benn went through a packed lobby and the door-keeper held out his hand to speak to him.

"'Mr Benn said: 'I have a certificate here which returns me as member for Bristol South-East.'

"'The door-keeper replied: 'You cannot enter, sir'.

" 'Mr Benn said: 'By whose instructions?'
" 'The door-keeper said: 'By Mr Speaker's instructions, sir'.

"Five minutes after questions time began Mr Benn entered the public gallery with his wife Caroline and his son Stephen, aged nine, and mother. They sat in the side gallery above the opposite side of the house.

"There was a storm of Labour cheers in the full chamber when the Speaker announced at the end of question time at 3.30 pm. 'I have been informed that Mr Anthony Wedgwood Benn this day desired to take his seat.

" 'I cannot admit Mr Benn to the chamber.'

And the unduly elected Bristol MP wasn't admitted until Lord Stansgate won his fight, was allowed to shed his peerage and became first Anthony Wedgwood Benn and then Tony Benn.

1962

The skyline of Bristol, historic city of hills, towers and spires, changed dramatically in the early 60s.

And 1962 was the year Bristol started to reach for the sky with the two first-ever 'skyscrapers' which would usher in two decades of building up and up and up. They weren't on the New York scale, but to Bristolians they looked like giants.

The printing company Robinson's space-age headquarters by Bristol Bridge was a whopper, a mega-block of light colour which stood out dramatically against its redbrick, low-rise neighbours.

Clifton Heights on the Triangle wasn't as big, bulky or tall but its position on the Clifton hillside made it visible for miles around.

High rise was a novelty when the Post sent reporter Roger Bennett to take a look at the two giants rising over the Bristol scene.

"Bristol's first two skyscrapers are racing neck and neck towards completion by next summer.

"In the middle of the city the £1 million Robinson Building is due for occupation in July, 1963.

"Overlooking it from the Clifton hillside three-quarters of a mile away, Clifton heights, 160 ft high and costing around £400,000, should be ready next June.

"The main structures of both buildings are now complete. Their full impact on Bristol's skyline can now be appreciated. Or not appreciated—depending on how you feel about these things.

"But nobody will quarrel with one thing. The views from them are absolutely magnificent. The Robinson typist and the Clifton Heights flat-dwelling tycoon will share the breathtaking daily experience of gazing out over a vast panorama of roofs and spires to green hills beyond.

"The Robinson office block has risen very quickly indeed. Demolition of the old buildings on the site by Bristol Bridge started in July last year, piling began in October and the building had risen to its full height of 15 storeys within a year.

"It will be one of England's first completely sealed, air-conditioned office blocks with an even inside temperature around the 70 degree mark.

"Despite the size of the project, there has been remarkable attention to detail. The young planning team headed by Robinsons' chief architect Mr John Collins, has wrangled long and often to make sure there is no jarring note design-wise. This goes right down to the shape and finish of salt cellars for the dining room and the style of lettering on lift buttons.

"Clifton Heights, towering above

The Robinson offices, Bristol's first 'skyscraper' block.

Triangle West, has been designed by 39-year-old Mr Raymond Moxley.

"He and Robinsons' John Collins are about the same age, are personal friends and work together on the board of Bristol Building Centre and the council of the Bristol and Somerset Society of Architects.

"It is a nice coincidence that they should together introduce Bristol to skyward building.

"The tower starts with a service area, then 10 floors of flats. Each floor will have five units, one with three bedrooms, two with two and two with one. Rents will range from £250 a year for the smallest lowest flats to £750 a year for the highest and largest.

"The top two floors will be let as a restaurant and bar where Bristolians will be able to dine overlooking the superb vista of the city".

53

1963

TUESDAY DECEMBER 17TH

No-one in Bristol missed the significance of the moment that bells chimed the hour for 8 o'clock that morning.

It marked the death of 23-year-old Russell Pascoe for his part in the murder of a Cornish farmer. Dennis Whitty, convicted with him, was hanged at the same moment in Winchester.

The execution was the last to be carried out in Bristol and one of the last to take place in Britain before the abolition of capital punishment in 1965.

The Bishop of Bristol, the Rt Rev Oliver Tomkins, who had earlier protested at the death sentence, visited the condemned man in his cells shortly before the hanging.

He emerged, pale-faced and weary, at the prison gates.

"Wearing his robes, the Bishop asked the 70 people keeping the silent vigil outside the grim prison walls to pray for the condemned man.

"But when he asked for 'a kind thought for the men who hate having to carry out this unpleasant task' a man shouted: 'They don't have to do it'.

"The Bishop replied: 'They do'.

"He went inside the prison 40 minutes before the time set for the execution—8 a.m.—and saw the condemned man.

"The demonstrators, who had kept up a day-and-night protest vigil since Saturday, bared their heads as the prison chapel clock chimed eight.

"At the same time Dennis John Whitty (22) was hanged at Winchester Prison for the same murder.

"Pascoe was visited last night by his wife and mother.

"Mr George Gummer, a Bristol accountant and local secretary of the National Campaign for the Abolition of Capital Punishment, said the Bishop had told them Pascoe was a changed man in the last three weeks—and one who had found the Christian faith.

"Mr Anthony Wedgwood Benn, MP for Bristol South East, who was outside the prison last night, thinks this will be the last execution in Bristol.

"He said: 'I am sure that in 1964 the death penalty will be abolished'.

"The last execution in Bristol was 10 years ago when John Owen Greenway of Swindon was hanged for murdering his landlady. The last in this country was in November last year at Strangeways, Manchester.

"Pascoe and Whitty, who had been living with three young women in a caravan near Truro, were sentenced to death at Cornwall Assizes for the murder of 64-year-old farmer William Rowe in the furtherance of theft.

"Their appeals were dismissed and on Saturday the Home Office announced that the Home Secretary had found no grounds to recommend a reprieve.

"The demonstrators at Horfield, who included university students and lecturers and a contingent who arrived from Cornwall last night, began to disperse shortly after 8 a.m.

"But one bearded youth shouted: 'Sickening. The people of Bristol should have torn the gates down instead of just standing around'.

"They left banners propped up against the prison gates. One read: "Let the Law of Kindness Know No Limits".

"Outside the prison, the campaign for the Abolition of Capital Punishment started a fund for the relatives of the dead farmer and the two men who murdered him.

"The Bishop of Bristol later issued this statement:

"Under the care of the prison chaplain,

Russell Pascoe asked for baptism and confirmation in the prison.

"So at the request of the governor and chaplain, I saw him on various occasions to offer my ministry and give him both his first and his last communion.

"I would have wished this, the normal ministry of God to His children in need, to be no more remarked upon than if he had been dying in hospital.

"But since it has become public, it will be of comfort to his fellow Christians to know that sin and shame were overcome.

"This victory no more justifies hanging than the fact that war may evoke heroism is a justification of war.

"But it is a reminder that no one is beyond God's reach."

1964

WEDNESDAY NOVEMBER 11TH

The Fab Four ended their all-screaming, all-raving 1964 tour in Bristol . . . and Bristol made sure that '64, the Year of the Beatles, ended with a bang.

Well, a rather soft bang as a joker turned the Liverpool lads who'd conquered the world of pop music into a whiter shade of pale that raucous night.

Mary Wells was also on the bill along with Sounds Incorporated, but Beatlemania was at its height and there were eyes only for the Four . . . including those of a daredevil prankster who crept into the ceiling space above the stage and waited for his moment.

"A practical joker risked his life last night to tip a packet of flour over the Beatles from the 50 ft high ceiling of the Colston Hall.

"The screaming audience went wild with delight as a great white cloud fell from the roof and covered John, Paul, Ringo and George with flour.

"With brilliant timing, it struck from above just as the Beatles hit the last chord of their greatest number, 'If I Fell'.

"The Beatles collapsed in fits of laughter, pointing at each other and dancing around the stage in stitches.

"There was flour in their hair, on their suits, in their guitars and all over Ringo's drums.

"Ringo turned his tom-tom upside down and shook it in a vain attempt to shake off the flour.

"Paul, bent double with laughter, grabbed the mike and shouted: 'It's the last night of the tour, you see' and broke into giggles again.

Paul McCartney and John Lennon at the Colston Hall, Bristol.

"The audience just sat roaring and shaking with laughter until the Beatles recovered enough to sing 'I Wanna Be Your Man'.

"But backstage, panic ensued. The mystery joker had broken the "foolproof" security system of the hall.

"Tour manager Mr John Clapton said: 'They are knocked out by the flour joke. They thought it was hilarious.

" 'I suppose it could have been another of the boys on the tour who did it but I have no idea who.' "

   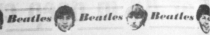

THEY SAID IT WITH FLOUR

Bristol really gets into the hair

A PRACTICAL JOKER risked his life last night to tip a bagfull of flour over the Beatles from a 50ft.-high ceiling of Bristol's Colston Hall.

The screaming audience went wild with delight as a great white cloud fell from the roof, covering John, Paul, Ringo and George with flour.

With brilliant timing, it struck from above just as the Beatles hit the last chord of their quietest number—if I felt.

The Beatles collapsed in fits of laughter, pointing at each other and dancing around the stage in stitches.

Giggles

There was flour in their hair, on their suits, in their eyebrows, in their guitars and all over Ringo's drums.

Ringo turned his tom-tom upside down and

● Jennifer Liley, of Southmead, gets with it at the Beatle Show. Below: a study in expressions.

REPORTS
by Evening Post pop reviewer
Roger Bennett

PICTURES
by Evening Post photographers
Erik Hansen,
George Edwards

banged it in a vain attempt to clean off the flour.

Paul, bent double with laughter, grabbed the mike and shouted: " It's the last night of our tour, you see " — then broke into giggles again.

The audience just sat roaring and shrieked with laughter until the Beatles recovered enough to launch into Ringo's song, " I Wanna Be Your Man."

Backstage, panic reigned.

Empty bag

The mystery joker had breached the "foolproof" security system in the hall. Every door to the roof was locked.

And manager Mr. Ken Cowley sent his staff on a lightning search for the culprit.

All they found was an empty flourbag lying on the plasterboard ceiling beside the hole through which the flour fell.

And all the evidence points to the culprit having been one of the Beatles' supporting turns.

A baffled Mr. Cowley said: " So far as I can see, that's the only answer. Nobody from outside could possibly have got up there.

" The joke itself was magnificent. The thing that worries me is that somehow our security measures were dodged.

" And even more worrying is the fact that the joker risked his life.

Danger

" One false step on to part of that slender ceiling and he'd have plunged 50ft. to the stage—possibly injuring one of the Beatles as well as himself.

" There are four ways up to the roof.

" One is from the back street. That door is still secure. One is through the battery room, that door is still locked and tied. One is from the dressing room, but the door lock is unbroken.

" The other is from the yard through the caretaker's flat, and anyone going through there would have been seen—unless, maybe, it was an artist who went unchallenged."

At the end of the show, the Beatles raced offstage and down to their waiting car, still smothered in flour.

Their manager, Mr. John Clapson, said : " They were knocked out by the flour joke. They thought it was hilarious.

" I suppose it could have been another of the boys on the tour who did it. But I have no idea who."

Whatever anyone else thought of the Beatles show the St. John Ambulance Brigade thought it was quieter than before. Their 18 ambulancemen and nurses standing by had an easy day's night with only 12 cases in the two houses.

One girl had an injured knee and was taken by ambulance to hospital for a check up, said Staff Officer C. Kimmings. The others just suffered from emotional stress.

● The "bomb" goes off, but the Beatles go on. Below: Paul McCartney and John Lennon in close harmony.

THEY CHARMED THE PARENTS, TOO

WHO SAID the Beatles were slipping?

Maybe the screams were just a tiny bit less ear-splitting than last year's.

But you don't expect mums and dads to scream. And quite a lot of Bristol parents enslaved tickets for last night's Colston Hall shows, having been won over by the teen Beatle charm.

The boys don't need gimmicks.

They just play and sing. And they are probably the only beat group in Britain who sound every bit as good live as on their records.

They aren't brilliant musicians. They haven't got marvellous voices.

" But they have got John, Lennon and Paul Mc Cartney's songs — the brightest, happiest, most catchy in the pop world today.

And just the right sound to sing them with.

Last night's programme was entertained by :—

A bagful of flour.

A cascade of jelly babies. Half a dozen fluffy toys, and 12 more collapsed with " emotional stress."

Three numbers were rockers the Beatles have

borrowed from other song-books and made their own — Twist and Shout, Money and Long Tall Sally.

The rest were all Lennon McCartney, from the wistful If I Fell, to the storming Hard Day's Night.

The rest of the show included some tuneful stuff from Brian Epstein's West Country stablemates The Koulks, mincing ballads from Miss Harlan, a bouncy performance from Tommy Quickly backed

by the Remo Four, and a welcome spot by American girl Mary Wells.

Mary was backed by Sounds Incorporated, Brian Epstein's most musically group who so far have apparently been too good to get in the charts.

But nobody could steal the show from the Beatles.

Maybe the beat boom is slipping.

But the Beatle boom isn't.

1965

WEDNESDAY APRIL 14TH

It should have been a day for motorists to celebrate in road-crazy Bristol.

After all, the city's leaders were demolishing Georgian relics on the edge of Broadmead as fast as they could to clear the way for the Bond Street dual carriageway.

Old Market was being dismembered for the great slice of underpass and bridgework to make Temple Way a swifter journey for the motorist.

There were firm plans to send a four-line motorway charging through inner suburbs like Totterdown, Clifton and Cotham.

And Bristol's proudest achievement, its very own spaghetti junction to make life easier for the commuters pouring in from the new satellite towns of Nailsea, Portishead and Clevedon, was being opened by Transport Minister Mr Tom Fraser.

Mr Fraser, however, wasn't in celebratory mood . . . he sounded more like a prophet of gloom.

"Transport Minister Mr Tom Fraser warned motorists that he is considering a 'congestion tax' to beat city jams.

"He is planning further steps to discourage people from using cars in and around city centres.

"Parking controls, loading and unloading and no waiting restrictions have to be used more strongly in the future, he said.

"Ships sirens hooted down the Avon Gorge as he opened the huge Cumberland Basin scheme this afternoon.

"Crowds cheered and motorists queued as Mr Fraser pressed the button to swing the bridge in favour of the vehicles.

"Then, at 12.30, precisely, the first car passed on to the concrete ramparts of this £2,650,000 road system.

"Motorists had been queuing back on to the Weston-super-Mare road and circulating around blocks in the Hotwells area, waiting for the barriers to be dropped so that they could be among the first to drive over the new swing bridge.

"Despite steady rain, scores of pedestrians swarmed across the bridge, which enables a new view to be enjoyed of the Clifton Suspension Bridge."

1966

THURSDAY MAY 19TH

Bristol . . . entertainments capital of the South West, and one of the entertainments attractions of Europe.

That was the talk of the town when Mecca moved into Bristol, splashed out a fortune and began building the New Entertainments Centre in Frogmore Street, towering over the ancient Hatchet Inn and the Georgian and Regency streets nearby.

The New Entertainments Centre wasn't just big, it was enormous and it was what 60s leisure and fun-time were all about, Mecca promised.

Here, slap bang in the middle of Bristol, the company was creating the largest entertainment centre in the whole of Europe.

A dozen licensed bars, an ice rink, bowling lanes, a casino, a night club, a grand cinema, a sumptuous ballroom and, naturally, a multi-storey car park to accommodate all those Zephyr Zodiacs, Anglias, Westminsters, Minis, Victors and Imps which would come pouring into town bringing the 5,000 or so customers who would flock to the centre every day.

London might have its famous West End. Bristol had its Frogmore Street palace of fun and the opening night of the biggest attraction of all, the Locarno Ballroom, on May 19th was the Night To Crown All First Nights, the Post proudly announced.

Sparkling lights, plastic palm trees in shadily-lit bars, a revolving stage, dolly birds in fishnet tights and grass skirts . . . this was glamour à la mid-60s and Bristol loved it.

Everyone wanted to be there on Night One but the guest list was limited.

It was, the Post reported the next day:

". . . a date to remember last night for 800 Bristol and West Country VIPs who saw the splendour of Mecca's new Locarno ballroom.

"At the New Bristol Centre were the mayors, the business chiefs and the top socialites of the city and neighbouring counties.

"Mecca, having spent £2 million on building, spared no expense in making the opening of the ballroom one of the gayest nights of the year.

"There was a gift of a commemmorative Churchill crown for every guest, including the Lord Mayor and Lady Mayoress, Ald. and Mrs Tom Martin.

"Ald. Wally Jenkins, chairman of the Public Works and Planning Committee, gave the ballroom Bristol's blessing in declaring the premises well and truly launched.

"When Mecca selected Bristol for their centre, they did not just do it with a pin, he said.

"They knew that Bristol deserved and

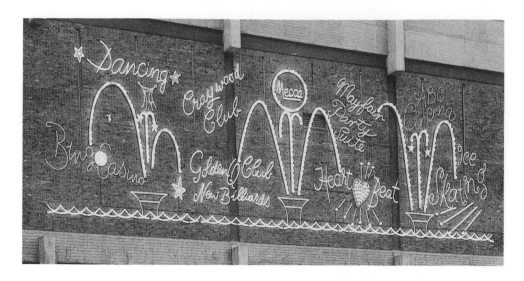

appreciated the best. Mecca had shown a swashbuckling and adventurous enterprise in providing it and Bristol would support it.

"To tell the guests last night all they wanted to know about Mecca, there were half a dozen hostesses, including winners of the West Country heat of the Miss Great Britain contest—in plumes, fishnet tights and bikinis.

"There were girls in grass skirts who brought on the pineapple confection for the buffet supper.

"There was Sidney Jones and his Orchestra playing conventional ballroom music and Wilf Ray and his Orchestra—including an ex-member of the Cadillacs, one of the West's top beat groups—playing superbly competent swing.

"There was glitter and glow of myriad lights.

"There was an atmosphere of rich opulent intimacy warming the place in a way not to be expected in a ballroom capable of holding more than 2,000 people.

"Guests were served drinks in the South Seas climate of the Bali Hai bar, in the swish Le Club bar and by check-waistcoated, bowler hatted barmen in the Victorian bar".

That was just for starters. In mid-November the Lord Mayor was there to open the magnificent £100,000 ABC Cinema at the centre. A week later Miss World, a beautiful Indian medical student, Reita Faria, came to town to open the Craywood Club, the new casino.

Bristol—Sixties entertainment capital of the West.

1967

In the big, big world of movies he was one of the greatest male stars, she was the greatest box office draw of them all . . . and together they formed a superstar pair which wanted Bristol as the TV jewel in their glittering crown.

The very mention of the names Richard and Elizabeth meant one thing in the Swinging Sixties. Richard'n'Liz, Burton and Taylor, Anthony and Cleopatra.

So it was front page news when it became clear that the most colourful couple in movieland's history were seriously contending to take over the TV franchise for Bristol and South Wales.

"Richard Burton told the Evening Post this afternoon: 'I am backing the bid for the West and Wales TV contract.

"'Both myself and Miss Elizabeth Taylor are strongly supporting this application' he said. Mr Burton is filming in Nice.

"He leads an international list of stars who have joined in the bid for the contract now held by TWW.

"Another star named today as "very interested" in the consortium bid is Harry Secombe. Film star Stanley Baker and opera singer Geraint Evans have already promised their support.

"Broadcaster Mr John Morgan, spokesman for the group, said this afternoon that Burton's involvement was "very considerable", both financially and in talent.

"He said Richard Burton was one of the originators of the £3 million bid to oust TWW after almost 10 years.

"Faced by a Saturday deadline for their application, the group are putting the finishing touches to their draft programme.

"Mr W.A. Hawkins, chairman of Bristol Evening Post, another group member, said: 'We have all the money we need. The emphasis will be on regional programmes of a high quality.

"'Important international stars will be used and there will be fewer quiz programmes. We shall keep some but they will be of a higher standard than the present programmes.'

"A statement announced: "The consortium has at no time sought any publicity for their application and has no desire to embarrass the ITA.

"'However, some details have been published and in order to clear up some speculation we would like to say Mr Richard Burton and Miss Elizabeth Taylor are strongly supporting this application. In fact Mr Burton is one of the originators." "

And they won. Bristol's telly company-owning superstars turned up the following year when TWW was given its marching orders and Harlech TV, later HTV, came into being.

She wore the biggest diamond ring anyone had ever see—'It's a present from Richard'—she announced—and HTV had the noisiest, best-publicised launch of all.

EVENING POST

No. 11,182—5d.   The paper all Bristol asked for and helped to create   Thurs., July 11 1968

Two dead and three others missing

KILLER FLOODS

Army rush aid to the West

A young Bristol man was swept to his death, an elderly woman was drowned and three people are missing in the floods which swept Bristol and the West.

It was the worst rainstorm to hit Bristol in more than 55 years, with more than five inches of rain falling in 24 hours.

This afternoon the Army were sending 30 amphibious vehicles to help in rescue work in Bristol and North Somerset.

And a team of engineers from Maidstone were to investigate the possibility of erecting a Bailey bridge at Pensford.

Those who died were:
Mr. George Christopher Bowden (38), of 189, Ashton Drive, who was killed in a bid to rescue two young women trapped to their necks in water in Hartcliffe Way; and

Mrs. Barbara Ward (85), trapped in a downstairs bedroom at her home at Sidbury Sidmouth.

WILLS BADLY HIT

The East Street, Bedminster, factory of W.D. and H.O. Wills suffered damage running into thousands of pounds, possibly six figures.

A large part of the stocks awaiting distribution, was destroyed.

So was a lot of tobacco leaf ready for processing.

Work in the factory was at a standstill, with several machines out of action (see also Page 9).

Work continued normally at Wills's two Ashton factories but East Street is their biggest concern in the city, employing 4,000.

NO POWER

The factory was without power and telephones but it was normal working for the office staff.

A spokesman said it was doubtful there would be a shortage of their cigarettes as they are also made at Wills's other factories.

But the East Street works are the sole producers of Golden Virginia tobacco and some pipe tobacco. If the shut down persists for any length of time, stocks of these could run short.

Employees of Wills's No. 1 Factory, East Street, are asked to report at usual time tomorrow for wages and further instructions. There will be no work for them in the factory, but clerical work will go on as normal.

Buses are 'booked'

Angry bus crews claimed late this afternoon that a traffic warden was going round Bristol's City Centre "booking" buses parked at stops.

"He's booked five so far," said one conductor Mr.

PAGE TWO ★★

Trapped

Among the missing and feared drowned are Miss Alexandra Giles (21), of Court Farm, Marksbury, and Mr. and Mrs. Charles Bernard Kaye, of Huddersfield.

All three were trapped in a car swept over a bridge at Keynsham.

Also in the car was Mr. Charles Kaye—son of Mr. and Mrs. Kaye and fiancé of Miss Giles.

He managed to escape in a bid to fetch help, but himself got into difficulties. He spent five hours stranded on a tree before being taken to safety in a dramatic rescue by the R.A.F.

This afternoon he was in Bristol Royal Infirmary, while Somerset police were making a massive search efforts for the missing car and its occupants.

For several hours police

PAGE TWO ★

BID TO BEAT BLACK-OUT

Round-the-clock electricity control centres were moved today into Bristol districts where thousands of people were blacked out.

South Western Electricity Board officials advised people in difficulty to contact their nearest mobile control or the central depot at Feeder Road.

The local controls are at Bedminster (off St. John's Lane), and Brislington (near the Ritz Cinema.

The worst hit district was Bedminster where three sub-stations were flooded and hundreds of homes without electricity.

Seven Bristol sub-stations were flooded last night and other supplies halted by lightning.

Other areas affected were Hartcliffe, Portishead, Keynsham, and North Stoke.

More than five feet of water flooded the Bristol district office of the South West Gas Board in Bedminster, causing considerable damage and putting the telephone exchange out of action.

A board spokesman said this afternoon that delays and inconvenience were inevitable, but a special phone number for emergencies—66-5131—is in use.

Church Street, Pensford, and a scene of chaos today as villagers tried to save a few belongings. This house in the street was ripped open by the River Chew, and only the bedroom was saved.

Road collapse

Bath Hill Bridge, Keynsham, the main thoroughfare through the town was closed to both traffic and pedestrians this afternoon after the roadway started collapsing into the river below.

See Page 2.

A family car, victim of the raging torrent which is sweeping down the gorge at Cheddar today.

Bid to prevent jams

Bristol police introduced a new traffic system this afternoon in a big bid to prevent huge jams, following the city's worst floods in living memory.

They began operating a huge circulatory system to help motorists get past Winterstoke Road, which is blocked by a quarter-inch stretch of water.

A Mini and several lorries are still submerged in the Ashton Gate underpass.

Traffic heading south of the A.38 was diverted to Cliff House Road, Cliff Road, North Street, Luckwell Road and back into Winterstoke Road.

Traffic heading north was diverted at Lidgate and across to the Weston-super-Mare road, to get to the city.

It was hoped to re-open East Street in time for the rush hour. East Street was a sorry sight this afternoon as traders cleared their shops of ruined stock (see page 9 for earlier pictures and report).

Nearly 300 Corporation workmen were helping with flood damage throughout the city.

Bristol M.O.H. Dr. Robert Wofinden said he was satisfied the city's water supply was in no danger and that boiling before drinking was no longer necessary.

1968

WEDNESDAY JULY 10TH

The rain began falling in the morning. At first it seemed like no more than a sudden summer storm. Cracks of thunder echoed across the Bristol region as the deluge continued . . . and continued.

By midday the rain was so persistent and severe that people sheltering from what they thought was a cloudburst had to abandon shelter and make a run for it, only to be soaked within seconds of stepping into the open.

By early afternoon it was becoming clear that this was something extraordinary. Post reporters were already filing tales of slight damage by the time that day's Three Star edition was being prepared.

There were already clear signs of flood damage to be seen across the city. Manhole covers were thrown into mid-air as drains failed to cope with millions of gallons of water from a downpour which went on and on and on.

Afloat in Lower Bristol Road, Bath.

Soaked . . . The Wills tobacco factory in East Street where 50 million cigarettes and 210 tons of tobacco were ruined.

That warm July evening brought no respite as the rain continued to pour down in the worst rainstorm the West Country had suffered for generations. There seemed to be no end to this storm.

Low-lying areas near the River Avon were particularly vulnerable despite recent efforts to prevent flooding. In other places the sheer volume of the water made a mockery of any drainage schemes.

Reporter Peter Thompson was sent to Brislington after an alert of potential tragedy. In the following day's Post he reported:

"At five past midnight I watched as two powered boats, one a fire service craft, the other private, rescued 18 people from the top deck of the No 339 Bristol–Bath bus.

"Around them in Brislington village square were cars which had disappeared beneath the swirling flood waters.

"The depth of the water was such that the 16 passengers, driver and conductor had no difficulty in stepping from the top deck emergency door into the boats.

"The problem had come in getting the driver on to the top deck. Eventually the conductor kicked in the front window to permit him to climb in.

"I met one of the boats on Brislington Hill as it brought ashore the conductor and six of the passengers.

"The conductor, Mr T. Gregory of Worcester Villas, Bath told me they had left Bristol at 10.05, arrived at Brislington at 10.25 and turned straight back to the depot for instructions. The orders given them were to attempt to get through.

"In a room of the White Hart Hotel a passenger, Mr M.C. Hill of Keynsham told me how as they entered the square, he had seen water up to the level of a dart board in one of the public houses. 'We knew we were in trouble' he said."

Five inches of rain—a month's average for a wet July—fell in little more than a day. Bedminster was flooded, Cheddar Gorge was transformed into a raging torrent and Keynsham and Pensford were torn apart by avalanches of floodwater.

Three people died when their car was washed away at Keynsham. In Hartcliffe a Bristol man died as he tried to save two young women trapped in deep water. The final death toll was eight and the cost of repairs to damaged buildings, ruined homes and broken bridges ran into many millions.

1969

THURSDAY APRIL 9TH

The Swinging Sixties went out with a dramatic roar in Bristol . . . and the world was there to watch the great event.

Tens of thousands gathered on every vantage point near Filton airport and an international audience of millions sat glued to their TV sets to witness one of the technological triumphs of the 20th century.

Concorde 002, the Bristol aviation industry's great white hope, was about to fly for the first time.

The development of the world's first supersonic airliner, built jointly in Bristol and Toulouse, had been dogged by political controversy, rising costs and fears for its future in a world that seemed to want hefty wide-bodied jumbo planes that carried lots of passengers rather than the slimline chic Concorde for the few.

But all those doubts were set aside shortly after 2 p.m. when test pilot Brian Trubshaw started up the ear-splitting shriek of the Olympus engines that powered the world's most exciting jet.

The ghostly, delta-winged plane slowly taxied to the Gloucester Road end of the Filton runway and then paused for the final checks.

The take-off at 2.24 p.m. was deafeningly noisy but smooth, with 002 rearing into the air and then gaining height to bank over the Severn before heading for RAF Fairford in Gloucestershire where it was to undergo lengthy tests.

Brian Trubshaw (left), Concorde Chief Test Pilot, and John Cochrane, Deputy Chief Test Pilot, on the flight deck of Concorde 002.

There were hundreds of TV and press crews at both ends of the short maiden flight. The *Evening Post*, which had backed the Concorde project from the start, was there in force.

The Post's man reporting the final moments of the historic event from Fairford wrote:

"About 200 press and cameramen who were at the end of the runway chased Concorde back to the silencing units in coaches.

"Then the gangway was wheeled to the Concorde door and there was a wait for the crew to emerge.

"Jubilant BAC officials joined several hundred pressmen in a celebratory toast of champagne. The crowd, estimated at 10,000 watched the aircraft land from the perimeter of the airfield.

"Brian Trubshaw walked down the steps from 002 and said: 'It was wizard'.

"Sir George Edwards, "father" of the project, commented: 'It was a jolly good moment to look back on'.

"And co-pilot Mr John Cochrane said: 'It was marvellous. We enjoyed every minute of it although it was a bit hot and sticky.

" 'We could not have been luckier in the weather. We were very fortunate in having such a nice day as this'.

And in a front page editorial, the Comment column pronounced:

"Concorde may have given us the runaround over the years, smitten us with fits of panic, temperament, wrath and fear, but 002's first take-off into the blue today makes all men love her.

"It is a matchless debut, reached through almost incredible tenacity of purpose and in the teeth of quite remarkable hostility. There will be unbounded joy and relief at Filton.

"Congratulations and thanks seem small words to offer to all who made her and to Brian Trubshaw who flew her. But they come with feeling from many thousands of hearts.

"Now, of course, Concorde has to prove that she is more than just a pretty airframe. She must be given every encouragement, from every quarter, to do so."

1970

SUNDAY JULY 5TH

It was the biggest, most romantic home-coming Bristol had ever seen and it was witnessed by hundreds of thousands who came not just from Bristol and the West but from all over the country.

And that was fitting. She was the *S.S. Great Britain*, after all, one of Brunel's masterpieces and a national treasure which was returning to her home port at last.

The Post had followed the fairy-tale story from the start, from the very first suggestion that the iron ship, the world's first propeller driven ocean liner, should be rescued from the Falkland Islands where she had lain a storm-battered hulk, used for storing wool and coal.

That daring rescue plan had first been put forward in the mid-1930s. It was only in 1970 that the dream came true, thanks to the Bahamas-based millionaire Jack Hayward, a man with a soft spot for Bristol and the Bristol Channel. First he had given £150,000 to secure Lundy Island for the National Trust . . . and then he had turned his attention to one of the most

Bristolians turn out in their thousands to welcome back Brunel's great ship.

famous ships to have sailed the Bristol Channel.

His donation of £150,000 to the rescue operation made it all possible. The hulk was raised on to a pontoon and on April 24th the mighty ocean-going tug *Varius II* began the long, long journey to bring back the *s.s. Great Britain*.

The Post's first sight of her came off Cornwall on Saturday June 20th when photographer Eddie Wood joined an RAF Shackleton crew on a search-and-find operation as the tug, pontoon and its rusty cargo reached the last lap of the marathon journey. The searchers divided their time between watching the radar screen and the sea below.

"It was three hours and several blips on the screen before a crewman called out 'I've got it . . . this is the one.'

"And it was. Down below, a seemingly empty sea was broken by two small flecks. We had found the Great Britain and the Varius II.

"Small, like toy boats on a pond, they seemed to barely move through the choppy grey-green seas.

"But as we closed in, the huge, red-rusty hull began to loom incredibly high as it rode the pontoon pulled by the tug."

Eddie Wood's excitement was just a tiny taster of what followed as first the *s.s. Great Britain* came into view along the Bristol Channel shoreline and then arrived triumphantly in Avonmouth on Tuesday June 23rd.

Jack Hayward was there to watch the fun as the *s.s. Great Britain* was gently eased alongside Avonmouth's North Wall. It was the start of a 12 day repair programme to prepare the great ship for being floated up the Avon to the dock from where she had been launched on July 19th 1843.

Jack Hayward said: 'I am very proud indeed. I have achieved the two projects which I felt were important for Britain'.

And then the greatest day of all when all the world watched the shabby, rusting remains crawl slowly up-river with its escort of three tugs.

Only 750 people were allowed on the Clifton Suspension Bridge, but it hardly mattered. The Avon Gorge provided spectacular viewpoints for all the huge crowds.

The *Evening Post*'s Phil Jones was among the select band allowed on the temporary deck to sail up the Avon on the ship.

"The real moment of history came as the Great Britain sailed majestically under that other of Brunel's masterpieces, the Clifton Suspension Bridge, which had not been built when the ship left Bristol.

"The crowds of cheering well wishers on the bridge rained confetti and flower petals on the convoy.

"Crowds packed both sides of the river and were jammed tight across the whole complex of the Cumberland Basin road bridge.

"People took to the rooftops and river banks to cheer the old lady on the last lap of her epic progress 8 miles up the Avon.

"Now she is back, snug in the dock of her birth, after the biggest maritime welcome in Bristol's living history."

1971

SUNDAY FEBRUARY 15TH

And then came that OTHER D-Day . . . the day that tanners and bobs, pennies and ha'pence, half crowns and ten bob notes were finally consigned to history.

D-Day was Decimalisation Day, the Monday that a confused Britain woke up to find that the coinage we'd known for centuries was a thing of the past.

New-fangled pounds worth 100 'pee' had replaced the familiar £1 which had been worth 20 shillings. The new 5p had replaced the old shilling which had been worth 12 pence. Sixpence had now become worth 2½p. The old penny wasn't worth anything.

Confused? If you are now, it was nothing like the chaos and confusion that came on the dawn of D-Day.

Lord Fiske, chairman of the Decimal Currency Board created to mastermind the change-over, spent the eve of D-Day in Harrods posing with a pair of Decibelles, two pretty girls trained by Harrods to help

customers with any troubles during the big day, while the store changed its cash registers.

In Bristol it was the same story as shops big and small spent that Sunday changing tills with the old pounds-shillings-and-pence registers to the new pounds-and-pees.

A confused public waited with apprehension and nervously clutched conversion tables when Monday came. The Board reassured shoppers with a list of Dos and Don'ts for D-Day.

". DO help the shopkeeper. If you don't have the right money, do as you've always done—give more and get the change.

". DO keep your decimal and £ s d coppers separate to avoid confusion. Pay decimal prices in decimal shops and £ s d in £ s d shops.

". DO think decimal. Once you have got the 'feel' of decimal prices, you can forget

£ s d.

". DON'T expect all shops to go decimal at once."

The Post's D-Day team were on the battle front that day. Jeremy Brien gave an up-beat picture of how the city had fared:

"Some grumbled. Some couldn't care less. And some even pretended it wasn't there.

"But for the majority of Bristolians, those 'damned dots' came in smoothly today.

"Newsagents, train booking clerks, shop girls and bank staff were all in the front line of the switch to decimal coinage.

"And although there were minor difficulties and some complaints, the general impression in Bristol was 'What's all the fuss about?'

"The big Bristol stores, which have been preparing the decimalisation path for more than six months, reported no major headaches.

"But there were some moans at neighbourhood shops away from the city centre.

"Mr Leslie Langdon said at the New Cheltenham post office and supermarket in Kingswood that his customers were calling the new coins 'dismal currency'.

"He added: 'They wanted to know whose idea the whole thing was and many of them said the new halfpenny was very small and would soon go out of circulation.'"

Meanwhile D-Day spawned the Decimal Dodgers, people who tried to use lower value new currency in slot machines.

Tough luck, Decimal Dodgers.

Machines like parking meters, laundromat washing machines and chocolate and cigarette dispensers quickly found out that the slots willingly accepted the half pence and 1p coins, but gave nothing in return.

And there was the tweed-suited, furious gent who flourished a tin of chicken curry at a Bristol shop counter as a Decibelle soothingly explained all the changes. He snorted: 'I'm just not interested in all this new-fangled decimal nonsense. Give me the change and forget the explanations.'

Bins of new pence at the Royal Mint at Llantrisant in South Wales ready to be bagged up for Decimalisation Day.

1972

MONDAY JULY 13TH

Up, up and away . . . they could have invented that phrase for the Bristol balloonist Don Cameron.

The quietly-spoken Scot had come to Bristol to work in the aircraft industry. He looked much more like a thoughtful school-teacher than one of the world's great aviation pioneers.

Though Cameron worked in the fixed wing aviation industry, his heart lay elsewhere. With lighter-than-air balloons. In 1966 he and some pals founded the Hot Air Group which produced its first balloon, The Bristol Belle, in 1967.

There were no licences for hot air balloonists then. Cameron argued that there should be and he won. Licence Number One was issued to one D. Cameron of Bristol.

Cameron Balloons began in the cellar of a house in Cotham in 1968 and he didn't do badly selling his products at £1,500 a time to well-off enthusiasts.

But Don Cameron had bigger ideas. He'd seen the crowds which gathered to watch his balloons inflate and rise at summer beanfeasts in and around Bristol and he was convinced that the big money future lay in promoting balloons as gigantic aerial advertising hoardings.

But how to make his balloons famous? By going for every record and publicity-seeking exploit he could.

And in 1972 the quietly-spoken Cameron stepped on to the world stage.

He started the year by soaring over the Sahara in a balloon. That sent the temperature soaring.

Then Don went for another big one—the world's duration record. To gain maximum publicity, he set off from the heart of Bristol. It was one of Cameron's rare but equally headline-making failures.

"Disappointed balloonist Don Cameron (32) vowed this afternoon that he would have another go on the world hot-air balloon duration record.

"He seemed undaunted after an emergency landing on a hill overlooking Hartcliffe Way, Bristol.

"He and his balloon Golden Eagle had been in the air only 1½ hours.

"The plan was to 'hang around' over Bristol for a total of nine hours to break the world record.

"'Of course I am disappointed—but I shall try again in the next couple of weeks' he said. 'I shall now have to wait for the right weather.'

"The emergency landing was made because of a leak in one of the massive balloon's fuel pipes.

"Mr Cameron had hoped to snatch back the accolade from American M.A. Wiederkehr, who recently took to the hot-air for 8 hours 48 minutes, three seconds.

"The dramatic ascent from the College Close at Clifton—in a balloon that cost £1,600 and is larger than the average house—even created a new entry in the cricket record book: Balloon stopped play.

"For even the participants in the annual Clifton College v. MCC match paused to watch the final stages as Mr Cameron heated the air with powerful gas burners".

A few weeks later Don Cameron won all the publicity he could have dreamt of. He achieved the first-ever crossing of the Alps by hot air balloon after being told it was an impossible journey.

Don Cameron and ballooning in Bristol had become world famous.

1973

TUESDAY APRIL 10TH

Shortly after 8 a.m. a cheerful group of passengers boarded an Invicta Airways Vanguard airliner at Lulsgate Airport.

Everyone was looking forward to an exciting day out in the pretty Swiss city of Basle ... groups of women like Congresbury Ladies' Skittle Team, family groups of mums and dads with their children and several mothers and children who had left dads behind, arranging to meet back at Lulsgate later in the day when dad had finished work.

Invicta's Basle excursion for shopping and sightseeing proved a winner with adventurous day trippers from Bristol and surrounding towns and villages. When the plane took off at about 8.30 a.m. it carried 148 passengers and crew.

At 10.10 a.m. Basle air traffic control lost touch with the pilot of the Bristol flight, code named Oscar Papa, on its landing approach. The plane had ploughed into a snowy, forested hillside near Basle, somersaulted and broken up.

Some in the rear section of the aircraft survived the crash almost unscathed and two, Bristol headmaster Barry Rogerson and a teenage boy set out to raise the alarm.

By midday news of the disaster had reached Bristol and the Post's air correspondent Malcolm Smith was on his way to Heathrow airport and to Switzerland. By early afternoon it was confirmed that more than 100 had died in the worst loss of life the Bristol area had suffered since the Good Friday blitz 32 years earlier.

In one heart-breaking moment fathers had lost their entire families, scores of children their mothers. The presence of so many groups of women friends and neighbours bore down heavily on small towns near Bristol like Axbridge, Cheddar and Congresbury where the day trip to Basle had been such an exciting date on the calendar.

Before that dreadful day was over, arrangements to fly relatives to Basle were already being completed. Within less than two days the heart-breaking task of identifying the victims had begun.

Malcolm Smith reported from the village of Dornach, near Basle:

"A boy of 14 from Somerset stood on the steps of the old school house here this afternoon and wept unashamedly, comforted by a woman officer of the Salvation Army.

"Inside the building he had just witnessed the most sobering of all moments—seeing laid in rows the dark-stained coffins of the victims of the Vanguard crash.

"It was the moment when my courage failed. I could not ask his name.

"This was his moment to be alone and the emotion swept through the small gathering of onlookers and the grey uniformed police who cast their gaze away from the pitiful scene.

"This is the darkest hour for the relatives and friends who faced the awful task of identifying their loved ones. It was harrowing to them all and they faced the challenge nobly.

"There was the impassive husband clutching a polythene bag with a coat and a handbag inside.

"There was the family group distressed but calm in the face of failure to find any clue which pointed to what happened to their daughter, an 18-year-old with a love of flying.

"Dornach this afternoon is bathed in sunshine. On the mountainside, still snow-covered a few miles away, lies the wreckage of Oscar Papa".

The final death toll was 108.

1974

WEDNESDAY DECEMBER 18TH

Bristol was in Christmas mood and the gaily decorated shops in Park Street had been bustling with Christmas shoppers in the final run-up to the holiday.

And then, at 7.30 p.m., came the call to Avon and Somerset police headquarters at Bridewell in the city centre. The telephone caller spoke with an Irish accent and said simply: 'In 20 minutes to half-an-hour a bomb will go off in Park Street'.

There were bomb hoaxes a-plenty that year as the mainland bombing campaign got into its stride. Explosions in provincial cities as well as the capital made police take every warning call seriously.

On the Avon and Somerset police patch, officers were even more rigorous after the region's first taste of terrorism came with a warning following by the blast of a 5lb bomb in The Corridor at Bath. That was just eight days before the Bristol phone call.

The pattern was the same as at Bath. The caller with an Irish accent. The lack of a code word. The threat was real enough.

Within 10 minutes of the alert 50 police officers were on Park Street, searching litter bins, dustbins, shop doorways and piles of wastepaper awaiting collection.

The search began at the bottom of Park Street and was making its way painstakingly up the hill when, at 7.54, there was the deafening roar and shockwaves of a device exploding outside Dixon's photographic shop further up the road. One man was hurt and taken to hospital.

The blast, the biggest bang suffered in the fashionable shopping street since bombs wrecked several shops during the blitzes of World War II, shattered plate glass shopfronts up and down the street.

Within a minute police had resumed their check of dustbins, doorways and other possible bomb hiding places. And

then, at 8.03 and without a warning, a second bomb exploded in a dustbin outside the Kenneth Harris hearing aid shop.

The muffled crump of the detonation could be heard two miles away. In Park Street itself the bang was deafening.

The second explosion seemed designed to catch police in the mop-up operation. In the event it caught a teenager hurrying to ring his and his girl-friend's parents to tell them they had not been hurt in the first attack. He suffered nasty burns and glass cuts. She was saved because he fell across her as shopfronts around them exploded in the shockwave.

In just eight minutes Bristol's premier shopping street had been reduced to a ghastly mockery of a Christmas attraction. Mercifully no one died, although 15 people were injured. The Post's six-strong team sent to the scene described the aftermath of the terrorist attack:

"A large facia above Kenneth Harris's hangs at a crazy angle. The force of the explosion blasted downwards into a cellar buckling a steel beam.

"The upward force has crumpled brickwork and a major re-building programme will be necessary.

"Across the road more shops ring to the sound of hammers and crowbars as glass clinging to broken frames is cleared for safety.

"A merry Christmas banner and silver tinsel, bathed still in an electric spotlight, looks incongruous flapping in the window of Rayner's Records where the smiling faces of Bob Dylan and Sir John Barbirolli appear on record sleeves—beckoning to the Christmas trade.

"At the Chapter and Verse bookshop, ironically, James Joyce's volume Dubliners stands unscathed and draws the eye from Sir John Betjeman portrayed on his dustcover with a stoic grimace.

"One wonders at the forces of science that in moments of explosion can cause such havoc yet leave seven milk bottles on a doorstep unscathed.

"One marvels at the way vast panes of glass can just disappear and at the force that drives the splinters to destroy furniture in the gaping front of an antique store.

"There is blood still on the pavement. It is a reminder above the clatter of the big clear-up that we are the lucky ones.

"The idiocy of the Park Street bombers has taken its toll in many ways and the faces are grim of those with a devilish task of finding the clues that led to the culprits."

1975

SUNDAY JULY 13TH

Hitched-up baggy trousers, basketball boots, tartan scarves, police, shrieking girls and near riots . . . you've guessed it. Rollermania was in town.

It came three times to Bristol in the summer of '75. There was the day they opened the box office at the Colston Hall for the forthcoming Bay City Rollers show. Then there was the dress rehearsal on May 29th when the band should have appeared but didn't. And then there was the real thing when the squeaky-clean popsters finally made it to Bristol and brought the house down.

The girl at the head of the queue at the Colston Hall when they opened the box office on May 8th was 16-year-old Rosemary Knight from London who'd

75

spent two days there. She'd already queued and bought tickets to see Rollers shows at Wolverhampton, Coventry and London and was going to see the band eight times on their '75 tour.

The queue veteran told the Post: " 'The only trouble was when some silly girl started saying that they were opening the box office early. Everyone started pushing forward and I was pushed into the glass door.

" 'The door broke on my knee but I wasn't hurt. Everyone's been very friendly here. I just wanted to see the Bay City Rollers. I'll go anywhere to see them.' "

But she didn't see them on May 29th when they were due. Lead singer Les Mckeown was involved in a fatal car accident in Edinburgh and the gig was postponed at the very last minute.

"News of the cancellation was flashed to the 100-strong police contingent detailed to safeguard possible troublespots.

"Police and ambulancemen at the city hotel where the group was due to stay, and the Colston Hall, relayed the news to fans.

"One officer said: 'They just wouldn't believe us. A few of them were crying and decided to go home but the diehard fans thought it was a ruse'.

"He pointed to one forlorn-looking 10-year-old girl in full tartan and ankle-length Rollers' gear and said: 'Just try to convince her that they aren't in Bristol. She simply won't believe it is true.' "

The show was re-arranged. The night the Rollers came to Bristol seven girls were taken to hospital from the Colston Hall—five were treated for hysteria, two for minor injuries—and another 40 were treated on the spot by the St John Ambulance Brigade while teeny and sub-teeny mayhem ruled.

The Post's Pop reporter, one James Belsey, wrote:

"The Rollers arrived on stage to the strains of the elegant Blue Danube waltz.

"The band smiled, waved, grinned, pranced around like puppets and danced like humans mimicking pogo sticks.

"They sang 'Shang A Lang', 'Be My Baby', 'Shout', 'Keep On Dancing' and, inevitably, finished the chaos with 'Bye Bye Baby'.

"They turned out some respectable guitar breaks, had a tight vocal sound and Les Mckeown radiated their cleaner-than-clean image with superb aplomb.

"Derek and Alan Longmuir, Eric Faulkner and Stuart Wood followed suit.

"The girls sang and screamed and fainted and the harassed, hot ambulance staff were rushed off their feet ferrying limp bodies to the safety of quieter corners.

"Music wasn't the point of the evening —it was a great big shouting, yelling, screaming, fainting thrill for the girls."

Later the final shrieks echoed away, the hall was cleared and it was all over. And Rollermania was over almost as quickly, as things turned out.

1976

WEDNESDAY APRIL 21ST

"They're Up! Bristol City have made it back to the First Division after 65 years.

"The 1-0 win over Portsmouth last night clinched it and ended the nervous anxiety, the heartaches and the worry of the last couple of months.

"Would they fold up at the final hurdle? Would there be a repeat of last season when they were all but there on Good Friday but dropped 3 points out of 4 in the home games against Norwich and Rovers and fluffed it?"

No they wouldn't, added Peter Godsiff, the man who'd been reporting City's trials and tribulations over the years.

The Post carried a four-page promotion supplement the morning after that famous Tuesday night as well as an electric match report and front and back page pictures of the aftermath . . . complete with a drenched, fully-clothed City manager Alan Dicks sharing champagne in the communal bath alongside his victorious players.

The Post was in no doubt that sporting big time would bring great changes the following season.

The editorial celebrating City's success was in breezy mood:

"It has been a long time coming. But perhaps the triumph of Bristol City's promotion to the First Division will taste all the sweeter for it.

"For years the soccer fan in Bristol has been denigrated for his lack of blind support for its teams, for the fact that he will not turn out to watch any opposition.

"But perhaps he has been maligned. Maybe discrimination has been confused with apathy.

"Next season should provide the proof. With Liverpool, Leeds and Manchester United on their guest list, Bristol City can honestly say their supporters won't see any better on the box.

"And maybe they will be in for a surprise. Perhaps this is what the football supporters of Bristol have been waiting for all these years and that closed gates will be the norm next season.

"Of course it could be just a pipe dream. But now is not the time to contemplate such things.

"Let's bask in the reflected glory of City's proud achievement. Let's cheer them to the echo. Let's give them the Freedom of the City.

"Make no mistake: First Division status means much more than better soccer in the city next season.

"It means the name of Bristol being blazoned further, wider and more often. We shall see more visitors . . . we shall do more trade."

Bristol City skipper Geoff Merrick kicking the ball around with youngsters after promotion to the First Division.

1977

FEBRUARY 4TH

Things that went bump in the night first annoyed then baffled Somerset and Bristol in the winter of 1976/77.

Not just bump . . . but Bump-Bump. On some nights the double detonation was heard from Taunton to Totterdown. What on earth was going on?

The story of those funny bumps started in Somerset in November, 1976 when folk living in North Petherton became alarmed by a double detonation that seemed to come shortly after 9 p.m. most evenings.

By November 14th they had called in the police, as the Post reported the next day.

"Inspector John Thouless of Sedgemoor police said: 'This is a very puzzling affair. The accuracy of the reports was completely confirmed by the constable we sent out to North Petherton to check.

"'We too have made widespread inquiries without result.

"'An extraordinary feature of the matter is that these regular rumbling noises have been reported from the Royal Ordnance factory at Puriton, Yeovilton, Wellington and even as far away as Crediton.' "

Locals had pointed the finger at both the Royal Naval Air Station and the ordnance factory. Not guilty, they said. They'd heard them too.

The Post made its own investigation and discovered that some of those mysterious bumps seemed to coincide with incoming transatlantic flights by British Airways Concordes. It didn't explain all the sounds, and anyway, BA said, their Concordes slowed down to subsonic well before reaching the coastline.

The Post dug a little deeper and found that some bumps came at about the time Air France Concordes bound for Paris were passing our shores.

A Civil Aviation Authority expert was sceptical. 'The usual carpet for hearing sonic booms is about 20 miles. At 30 miles the sound has disappeared or very nearly so. Yet this noise is being heard at far greater distances'.

At which point Bristol University decided to step in to nail the noise once and for all. A group sat in Somerset gardens, recorded the sounds and went to work.

On February 4th, 1977, they were ready and they called a press conference. The Bump Boffins pinned the blame for disturbing the peace of the West Country evening firmly on Bristol's wonder plane.

"As Concorde approaches Europe—both Air France flights to Paris and British Airways flights to Heathrow—it flies supersonic until within 40 miles of coastlines.

"But before the plane decelerates to subsonic speeds it is making the typical double bang sonic boom heard from all supersonic planes.

"And that bang bounces—either off the sea and strong upper atmosphere winds or off the strong upper atmosphere winds directly—and comes back to earth giving the typical deep rumble of the Somerset bumps.

"Dr Tom Lawson, reader in industrial aerodynamics said: 'Of 584 reports from the public, only about a dozen people were concerned or worried'.

"He said the pressure of the Somerset Bumps was equivalent to the pressure of an object travelling at 2 mph—and the sound is the equivalent of a car door slamming about 50 yards away."

So now we knew . . .

1978

MONDAY JULY 24TH

On July 24th, shortly before midnight, a daughter was born to John and Lesley Brown of Hassell Drive, Easton, Bristol.

Baby Louise weighed in at 5lb 12oz and this time when the Post, like every newspaper in the country, described the new-born infant as a "miracle" babe, it was hardly less than the truth.

She would have been a miracle even a decade before. For the tiny Bristolian was nothing less than the world's first test tube baby.

Louise was delivered in hospital at Oldham where the Browns had travelled to be under the care of the famous gynaecologist Mr Patrick Steptoe who had predicted in 1970 that the first test tube baby would be born "next year".

That announcement was rather over-optimistic, as things turned out. But for childless Lesley Brown, it was well worth the wait when she became one of his patients.

These days the fertilisation technique pioneered by Dr Steptoe and first brought to a successful fruition with little Louise's birth has become an accepted part of medical practice. In 1978 the story of the Browns was a wonder which brought a sudden ray of hope to countless childless couples.

John and Lesley had tried for children for eight years when Dr Steptoe was approached. He found Lesley had a fault in her fallopian tubes. So fertilisation was made in an intricate piece of medical

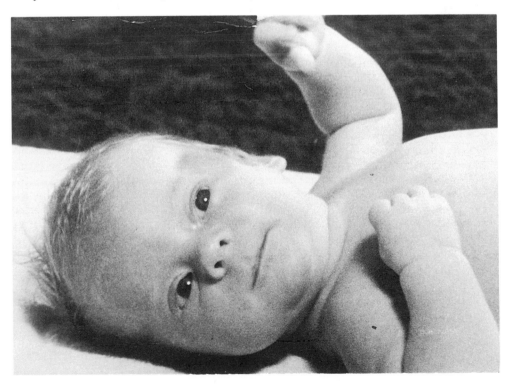

glassware ... and the fertilised egg successfully re-implanted in the mother-to-be's womb.

The experiment had been attempted many times and failed. This time it worked brilliantly.

The next day's *Evening Post* front page headline summed it up:

Mrs Brown You've Got A Lovely Daughter.

"The world's first test tube baby snoozed peacefully in a plastic cot alongside her overjoyed Bristol mum this afternoon.

"Staff at the Lancashire hospital said mum and baby were both 'excellent'.

"One member of the health department crew who filmed the birth said: 'She is a beautiful baby.

"'She's got a very small amount of hair and she certainly did a lot of bawling and crying as soon as she was born'.

"The baby was just over a week premature and was delivered by caesarean operation by Mr Patrick Steptoe, the gynaecologist behind the epoch-making step in medical history.

"Mrs Brown's husband, Bristol railway worker John (38), was driven to the hospital last night and afterwards held the wonder baby in his arms.

"He said: 'I am so happy I could cry. It was just like a dream'.

"In fact there were plenty of tears from the thrilled father and one hospital worker said: 'I have never seen a man so excited. He was laughing and crying at the same time . . . he was choked with joy.'"

John and Lesley Brown's joy didn't end there. Four years later Lesley gave birth to her second test tube daughter and this time the delivery was made at Bristol Maternity Hospital. Delivering test tube tots had already become part of a hospital's routine.

1979

MONDAY APRIL 2ND

T-Day, the day Margaret Thatcher came to power, was only a month away but everyone forgot politics and General Election campaigning the morning Oxford University's Dangerous Sports Club came to town—and won themselves a place on front pages across the world.

Their plan? The most outrageous, daredevil April Fool's Day stunt of them all.

The club's most reckless members were planning to jump off the Clifton Suspension Bridge. And they succeeded.

The next day's Post reported:

"Four daredevils jumped off Clifton Suspension Bridge as an April Fool's Day stunt—and lived to drink a champagne toast dangling halfway down the Avon Gorge.

"The four—all members of the exclusive Dangerous Sports Club—took the terrifying 250 ft plunge with only two-inch thick elasticated ropes between them and a sticky end in the murky waters of the River Avon.

"Nothing had been left to chance in planning the carefully-detailed stunt, except whether the 100ft ropes would be strong enough to hold them as they plummeted down at 50 mph.

"The only practice jumps they had done were from a tree in a friend's garden.

"Police and the Bridge authorities had been tipped off earlier that a stunt was

Top-hatted David Kirk, holding a bottle of champagne, makes his leap from Clifton Suspension Bridge.

Houses pose a problem

Fearless four take a dive

By DAVE BAXTER

Four daredevils jumped off Clifton Suspension Bridge as an April Fool's Day stunt — and lived to

The daredevil leap as seen in that day's Post.

planned and security was tight as the jump deadline of 6 a.m. passed without incident.

"Then, shortly before 8.30 a.m., three cars drove on to the bridge from Clifton and the four leapt out. They quickly secured their harnesses and fixed the ropes to the Bridge supports.

"Cheered on by friends from Oxford and Bristol Universities, expedition leader David Kirk, Alan Weston, Simon Keeling and Tim Hunt, younger brother of racing driver James Hunt, dropped the ropes over the side.

"Lecturer Mr Kirk was the first to jump, wearing morning dress with a topper strapped under his chin and clutching a bottle of champagne for luck.

"Simon Keeling (22) another Oxford post-graduate followed with diplomat's son Alan Weston (23) close on his heels.

"Tim Hunt shut his eyes before jumping and then all four dangled patiently waiting to be hauled up as police closed the bridge to traffic for 20 minutes.

"One spectator, Mr Nick Barrett, an Oxford student, said; 'They must have bounced down about 200 feet and then up to 70 feet and then down again.'

"All four were then taken to Southmead police station—Simon nursing a bruised jaw after the rope hit him on his way down.

"Later David said: 'It was a wonderful experience, very exhilarating.'

"The Dangerous Sports Club chose the Clifton Suspension Bridge—Britain's highest suspended span—because nobody had staged a controlled jump there before."

1980

The 1980s was less than two months old when Bristol had something very special to celebrate . . . and the confirmation that its best-loved star since Cary Grant really was the greatest.

Robin Cousins took the Gold Medal in figure skating at the Lake Placid Winter Olympics—and he kept the nation awake throughout the night to see if he really could become the champion.

Robin, the boyish 22-year-old from Sea Mills, had made steady progress through the skating scene. From a precocious youngster who'd showed rare skills as a novice at the Silver Blades ice rink in Bristol, he had developed into a skater with an extraordinary dramatic talent as well as a superb technique.

It was a heart-stopping blend of athleticism and artistry and the world was at his feet when he took to the ice in the final moments of the Olympic challenge.

He skated brilliantly, pipping the East German Jan Hoffman by the narrowest of margins to take the Gold Medal and achieve his lifetime's ambition.

He didn't know whether he had won until a moment before the presentation ceremony, as millions of British fans could see as they watched the final on early morning TV.

'It was an incredible feeling when I realised I had won' he said minutes later. 'I couldn't believe it.

'My feet weren't attached to the rest of my body and I literally tripped on to the rostrum.'

Back home there were cheers and huge sighs of relief when those marks went Cousins' way that early morning.

The Post kept an eye on Robin's neighbours to see how their night had gone.

"Bleary-eyed residents of Dingle Close, Sea Mills, Bristol, where Robin and his parents Fred and Jo live, are recovering from an all-night TV viewing session of the Lake Placid event.

"Next-door neighbour Mr Douglas Cotterell stayed up until nearly 4 o'clock this morning to watch Robin's victory.

" 'I was on the edge of my chair all night' he said.

" 'When he first started skating all those years ago I never dreamed he would win the Olympics.

" 'But he and his parents have worked incredibly hard for this and he's a very nice lad—I can't think of anyone who deserves a medal more.

" 'I expect the Close will be celebrating this in some way.'

"Sydney and Audrey Thompson, who have known Robin all his life, were also over the moon. But they didn't watch him win.

" 'We were really tired last night but we knew he was going to win anyway' said Mrs Thompson.

" 'It's funny to think the little kid who used to play next door is now a world skating star. This is a great honour for Bristol and for the Close.'

"Robins's victory did not go unnoticed elsewhere in the city.

"Window dressers started work on a special victory display at Sue Sheppard's Park Street Staff Bureau at 5 a.m. today.

"The display in giant letters, said: "Well done Robin".

" 'We planned it a long time ago in the hope that Robin would win' said Miss Sheppard. 'Now he has honoured the city in this way I hope that other traders will be doing the same sort of thing.' "

*Above: Robin acknowledges
the crowds on his triumphant
homecoming.*
*Left: Seen at Lake Placid
during the skating programme
which won him the coveted
Olympic Gold.*

Love it or hate it, the Spectrum building soon became a Bristol landmark, especially at night.

1981

THURSDAY OCTOBER 22ND

The Dallas look in Bristol? It certainly sounded like it the day the Post revealed plans for the city's most unusual office block.

The site was of huge importance . . . slap bang at the end of the M32 motorway and its dual carriageway extension which brought visitors whizzing straight into the heart of Bond Street and Broadmead.

It was THE prestige site and it demanded something very special.

On October 22nd the Post reported:

"One of Bristol's biggest-ever property deals, a £15 million office and flats project, was unveiled today.

"The glass fronted seven-storey office block would look out on Bond Street and the Broadmead shopping area and stand at the corner of Newfoundland Street.

"If the suggestion that 'mirror' glass be used is accepted, it would make the building one of the most unusual and exciting in Bristol.

"At developers Espley-Tyas today, it was said the scheme would bring to Bristol a major, prestigious complex providing the type of accommodation 'normally found in central London but at half the cost to the occupiers.' "

The Spectrum building opened on October 4th, 1984 and was in trouble from the start. Some loved it, including the Post's architectural correspondent Michael Jenner, some loathed it, like Avon's planning committee chairman Don Dolling who took a leaf out of Prince Charles' book by slating such hi-tech modernism as a 'glass monstrosity . . . if that is modern architecture, I'm sorry someone should have that point of view'.

Then Spectrum failed to find tenants. Then those famous mirror glass windows started picking up nasty stains from the heat of the sun, so Bristol University expert Steve Lubetkin, son of one of the world's most famous modernist architects Berthold Lubetkin, who also lived in Bristol, was called in to devise a method of removing the stains.

After two empty years the first occupants arrived. Five years after the official opening ceremony, Spectrum was working at full stretch at last.

On March 13th 1989 the Post reported:

"Spectrum, Bristol's futuristic office building which opened in 1984 and for a time seemed destined to become a 'blue' elephant, is now fully let.

"For the first two years no tenants could be found for the attractive glass-house that is illuminated in blue at night and lends an air of Dallas to the inner-city ring road at the mouth of the M32.

"Then the city council's development office was invited to move in rent-free.

"This was a wise move because it meant representatives of firms wishing to move to Bristol had to call at Spectrum—and their visit was an eye-opener.

"Eventually the economic development office had to move out to make way for other tenants. Spectrum has become the place to be."

1982

Ashton Gate had never seen a crowd like the one which made the pilgrimage to Bristol City's football ground the day the Rolling Stones and their entourage swept into town to give Bristol a blast of their rock'n'roll past.

The Stones were no strangers to Bristol. They'd played the Colston Hall in their heyday in the Sixties—and been turfed out of the dining room at the Grand Hotel when a young Mick Jagger arrived wearing a grey sweatshirt and jeans.

The dress code was an inflexible one back in the Sixties and the Grand's manager didn't give a damn for Mr Jagger or his beat group, as they were called in those days. He was shown the door, Brian, Bill, Keith and Charlie followed him and the Stones ended up eating curry in a restaurant in Park Street.

They were back at the Colston Hall in 1971, rich, resplendent and already respectable with a backstage parade of superbly dressed wives and girlfriends like Bianca Jagger and a cornucopia of delicious, artistically arranged food and drink to please their tastes.

Eleven years later stadium rock, an American creation involving massive concerts in the biggest open air venues available, had crossed the Atlantic and the Stones—by then pillars of the older rock'n'roll establishment—latched on to this lucrative showbiz market gleefully with a lavish tour of brightly staged mega-shows to pull in the punters.

The Bristol gig was an on-off affair until a few weeks before the main event. Too noisy for a Sunday, locals said. Then the authorities relented, ticket sales went wild and at last the Stones arrived to do the business.

"It needed more than a brief downpour to dampen the spirits of 36,000 passionate

Mick Jagger in Bristol.

Rolling Stones fans as Mick Jagger and Co played their first Bristol concert for 11 years.

"The seething crowd, packed like sardines on to the pitch and crammed into the terraces on three sides of Bristol City's

Ashton Gate ground, were never going to let a spot of bad weather take the edge off the jubilant proceedings.

"They arrived in marvellous humour. They sang, clapped, danced and chanted with all the gusto they could muster.

"The weather stayed kind throughout the warm-up proceedings. Indeed, the Stones were half-way through their long show when dark clouds rumbled overhead and the rain came down.

"Jagger himself remarked on the ill luck, pointing out that he was quite likely to end up on his backside if he kept on racing like a teenager around the slippery, sloping stage.

"But nothing could deter the band or their legions of passionate followers. The crowd response gathered momentum through the downpour and by the time the Stones launched into their old classics, the sun was out again.

"And when Mick Jagger tore off his T-shirt to wild applause, it was too much for one well-endowed young lady who decided to follow suit. She danced topless directly in front of her idol.

"The fans were by no means all from the West. Many had made long trips from the north, Midlands and Wales.

"Life-long Stones fan Paul Merrett from Hereford said: 'There was no way I could get tickets for the Wembley concerts, so when I heard about the Bristol gig I got down here as quickly as possible and queued all night.

" 'To be honest, I don't reckon the band are as good as they were 10 years ago. But that doesn't make any difference, because they're still the best and you don't know if you'll ever get a chance to see them again'.

"The band received a five minute standing ovation before they returned for an encore to play their most famous number, Satisfaction.

"The curtains were pulled back again to reveal Jagger chanting the words from a hoist platform which moved out directly over the heads of the front of the audience.

"In true Stones tradition, they went out with a bang. As they left the stage, a deafening fuselage of fire-crackers, rockets and smoke bombs was set off behind the stadium."

And, in true Stones tradition, they cocked a snook at authority even in their middle age. Locals in Ashton and Bedminster hadn't minded the sound of the music . . . but that ear-splitting finale of explosions was too much.

It caused so many complaints that Bristol City Council decided that never again would Ashton Gate be granted permission for a mega-rock show.

Ron Wood (left) and Keith Richards at Ashton Gate.

1983

FRIDAY JUNE 11TH

"Tony Benn hinted that he would be looking for a political future outside Bristol after his defeat in yesterday's General Election.

"Mr Benn, who has been an MP in the city for 33 years, lost in Bristol East by 1,789 votes.

"He left the count to cheers from his supporters while newly-elected MP Jonathan Sayeed walked out almost unnoticed.

"Mr Benn went off to a private party at Transport House in Bristol almost immediately after his defeat.

"He told the assembled crowd outside Brislington School: 'I would like to thank the people of Bristol who, for a third of a century, have returned me to Parliament.

"'I would like to tell them how glad I am that I stayed. Nothing but the decision of the people of Bristol that someone else should represent them would have induced me to leave this city.

"'Nobody should be discouraged by this result and I hope nobody will weep for me'.

"Insurance broker Mr Sayeed (35), who was fighting his first Parliamentary election, said: 'I would like to congratulate Mr Benn for sticking to his guns and not running to a safe Labour seat.'

"Mr Benn looked cheerful while the result was announced but tears welled up in his eyes when a chant of 'You'll be back' went up.

"The Post's Political Editor Michael Lord writes:

"The love affair between Tony Benn and Bristol is over, 33 years and 13 elections after it began.

"It took a succession of boundary changes, a huge Tory swing, Liberal intervention and a collapse of public faith in Labour to cut the link between the city and Britain's most controversial politician.

"He could have had any number of safe Labour seats but was determined to give the people of Bristol East the final decision on his future.

"Tony Benn, who chose to stand and fight, is out and the Commons has one radical thinker fewer."

Packing his bag . . . Post photographer Richard Mitchell's study of Tony Benn's departure from the election count.

1984

APRIL 9TH

Derek Robinson, well-known author, broadcaster and later *Evening Post* columnist told the *Evening Post* not many weeks before that Horton was one of those places where nothing had happened for the past thousand years and nothing would happen for the next thousand years.

The Bristol-born top thriller and war story writer who had made his home in the hamlet near Chipping Sodbury couldn't have been more wrong.

On the morning of April 9th farmer's wife Maggie Backhouse, aged 40, climbed into the family Volvo estate at Widden Hill Farm in Horton to set out for supplies from a local vet. The car exploded.

The Post reported:

"A village vendetta led to farmer's wife Mrs Maggie Backhouse being injured in a car bomb explosion at her home in Horton, near Bristol, today.

"She was taken to Frenchay Hospital where she was undergoing surgery this afternoon.

"Mrs Backhouse managed to stagger from the car. She was seen by passers-by at 8.20 this morning. The farm was immediately cordoned off and sniffer dogs were used to scour the area.

"Detective Superintendent Tom Evans, leading the inquiry, said the family had been receiving threatening anonymous telephone calls.

" 'There has been a recent history of anonymous phone calls to the home threatening the husband and the family. The police are investigating' he said.

" 'A lamb's head was found with a message which gives us reason to connect it with the telephone calls'.

"Mrs Backhouse and her husband Graham, aged 44, are well liked, villagers said today.

"Local author and neighbour Mr Derek Robinson said: 'Hearing of a car bomb in Horton takes my breath away. I can't believe it has happened to Maggie—she is a typical farmer's wife.' "

The Post was back in Horton three weeks later on the morning of May 1st. This time someone had been killed.

"Police called on villager Mr Colyn Bedale-Taylor only hours before he was found shot dead at the home of hate-campaign victim Mr Graham Backhouse in Horton last night.

"Today Det. Chief Supt. Alan Elliott said the police visit was a pure coincidence although former Army officer Mr Bedale-Taylor, aged 63, had been interviewed more than once over the bombing.

"Last night police called to Widden Hill Farm found Mr Bedale-Taylor dead with gunshot wounds and Mr Backhouse with stab wounds to his face and body.

"Mr Backhouse had been guarded by police after the bombing incident. It was called off at Mr Backhouse's request on April 19th.

"Both Mr and Mrs Backhouse are now under police guard at Frenchay Hospital."

Later Graham Backhouse was arrested after police pieced together the full story of how he had fallen into debt, attempted to collect £100,000 by murdering his wife with a bomb and then shot dead his neighbour Colyn Bedale-Taylor hoping to make him the scapegoat.

The sheep's head, the telephone threats and the rest of the "vendetta" had been a deception. The deception, like the bizarre insurance fraud, failed fatally.

Backhouse was sentenced to life imprisonment.

Above: The threatening letters shown to the public. Left: The scene of the crime.

1985

It was the most public John O'Groats to Lands End walk for decades . . . and when the Ian Botham Roadshow arrived in town, Bristol gave the West Country's favourite Bad Boy/Good Guy a hero's welcome.

The story had begun in the West Country—when Botham had accepted an invitation to visit children suffering from leukaemia in Somerset during his days as one of the Taunton-based stars of the Somerset Cricket Club. He vowed to help and decided that a sponsored walk would be his gift. He was joined by three friends, sports journalist Chris Lander from the Chew Valley, John Border, brother of Australia's cricket captain Alan and Phil Rance, who all started on Day One.

And the story reached its triumphant finale in the West Country. From the moment that Ian Botham stepped into the *Evening Post*'s circulation area near Stroud on the A38 in the final marathon leg of his tip-to-tail trek through Britain, he knew he was among friends.

The Bristol leg of his giant stride was a day-long march from Newport, near Dursley, on the A38 and then along the main road through Almondsbury, Filton, Bishopston, Stokes Croft to the centre before continuing up through Bedminster and Bedminster Down to Lulsgate. A total of 28 miles.

"Botham's funny hat stood out like a beacon as he prepared to take on the full force of fan worship from onlookers of all ages as he approached Bristol.

"He talked about the daily routine of his marathon trek with its unbroken discipline of four miles an hour for seven hours.

" 'We find it easier to think of hours' he said. 'Rough times? Yes, we have had some and we did try too hard at first when we were doing 35 miles a day.

" 'Once it is over at the end of each day, we'll sit around, our special POW T-shirts on—the four Prisoners of the Walk—and have a drink'.

"One of his fellow POWs, Manchester hairdresser Phil Rance—Phil's wife Lin comes from Pilning, said: 'Both has been great. The public don't see the side of Both we have seen and we have got to know each other well.

" 'If one of the four is having a hard time, we instinctively know it and there's always support from each other'.

"By the time the procession arrived on the outskirts of Bristol, the crowds were getting bigger, the walk more hurried as teenagers bustled and danced and pushed their way into the column."

Botham brought Bristol to a halt as the march went through town. Tens of thousands cheered and urged him and the procession onward and Botham, for once, looked stunned.

The next day's Post reported from Lulsgate as the walk headed further south . . . and after the donations on the Bristol leg had been counted.

"Bristol has proved to be the most generous place so far on Ian Botham's charity walk.

"A total of £26,808 was donated on the 27th stage of his 870 mile walk . . . and yesterday's greetings from Bristol gave the Somerset star enormous pleasure.

"He said: 'It was the best reception I've had so far. What a great day!' "

1986

Archie Leach fled Bristol as a stage-struck teenager, became Cary Grant in Hollywood and was one of the brightest stars of the golden age of Hollywood.

He was the epitome of screen elegance, witty, urbane, dashingly handsome, a man for every romantic part.

Cary's love affair with Bristol lasted and lasted. Although he made his home in California, he came back to the West Country year after year, first on ocean liners, then on the early intercontinental prop airliners which had to break their journey in Iceland to refuel and finally on today's familiar jetliners.

The morning after his death in America, the Post's veteran showbiz writer and diarist Alston Thomas could at last write about the Cary he knew.

"I knew him for the better part of four decades and for some years lived a few doors away from his late mother, Elsie, in Coldharbour Road, Redland.

"Towards me he was always kind but not unduly friendly. I was one of two journalists entrusted with his private bedside telephone number at his California home.

"There were times when he was most communicative, others when he was taciturn to the extreme.

"He struck up what, for such a private character, was a special relationship with Bristol newspapers after an unfortunate altercation at the funeral of his father, Elias Leach, during which a photographer's camera was damaged.

"He promised to tip them off whenever he came to Bristol. He posed for a few pictures and gave brief interviews.

"In return, pressmen promised never to pester his mother for her views on her famous son's career and his many romances.

"She was easily confused by strangers and he had a dread that his fans would learn she had spent some years in a mental hospital.

"Although it was difficult to do so unnoticed, he enjoyed visiting the Bristol Hippodrome where he had made his Bristol debut as an acrobatic dancer in August 1918.

"Earlier he had worked as a stagehand at the Empire Theatre in Old Market, Bristol.

"His last act in connection with his native city came in April when he broadcast the weekly radio appeal, Week's Good Cause, on behalf of the University Settlement, Barton Hill.

"It brought one of the biggest responses the programme had known and donations poured in from all parts of Britain and the continent.

"His fear of becoming old was almost an obsession and he hated to talk of death. He refused to celebrate his 80th birthday although he admitted to having been deeply touched to receive the 80th birthday greetings from the Lord Mayor of Bristol.

"All his life he boycotted television. When it became the major entertainment media 30 years ago, he vowed never to get involved.

"He saw it as a threat to the film industry, to which he owed everything, and to his close friends in movies.

"The BBC in Bristol had planned to bring him back to the city for a major documentary on his life to mark his 80th birthday, taking in his birthplace in Hughenden Road, Horfield, his old school and many other places associated with him.

"But he refused to co-operate and the venture was abandoned.

"Evening Post photographer Jack Garland probably got on better with Cary

Jack Garland's classic 1950s picture of Cary at the bus stop in Coldharbour Road.

Cary Grant poses for the photographer on a visit in 1969.

Grant than other newspapermen.

"Cary took Jack's phone number with him around the world and frequently called him.

"One dismally dull day in August 1965, when Cary had just married Dyan Cannon, Jack received a call from Cary which simply said: 'I'm on my honeymoon. If you're at the top gate of Bristol Zoo at 11.30 you'll see a tatty old Austin Cambridge. My cousin, (the late Eric Leach) my new bride and I will be in it.'

After posing with his bride, Cary drew

Jack aside and whispered: 'You've got the only honeymoon pictures. You could make yourself a lot of money.' "

Sadly for Jack, when he returned to the office the then editor of the Post was so delighted with the scoop that all the pictures and negatives were seized so that they could not leave the office.

Cary said later: 'It was a great pity. I only wanted to do Jack a favour. I could always trust him and wished to show my appreciation.'

1987

FRIDAY JULY 17TH

Buy your own home . . . and join the property boom! That was the message everyone was receiving in the mad, mad, multi-billion home buying spree of the late 1980s.

One subject dominated conversations that summer. How much houses were worth today, how much they had cost yesterday and what they would be worth tomorrow. No wonder it was front page news.

And there was a new breed of buyer who came singly or in couples to join or cash in on the new opportunities the spiralling prices offered.

Bristol began to hear more and more about the Yuppie, the Young Urban Professional and the Dinkies, the Double Income No Kiddies duo who were setting the pace in the big scramble for that dream home of your own.

On July 17th the Post gave the final confirmation that things were out of hand: **Home Boom Goes Crazy** the front page banner headline read. It was true.

Under the headline the Post's chief reporter Martin Powell wrote:

"The property market in Bristol is now so buoyant that one man has just spent two days queuing for a flat that he may sell without even moving in.

"Mr Paul Hamblin and Mr Chris Merrick have slept on the pavement for two nights to buy a studio flat overlooking Bristol's water-front.

"Four flats in the Buchanan's Wharf complex in Redcliffe were released at 9 a.m. today and were immediately snapped up—they could have been sold ten times over.

"Mr Hamblin started queuing on the pavement on Wednesday determined to be the first in when the doors opened today.

"The one-bedroom studio flats are being sold for up to £55,000. A £69,000 two-bedroom flat has been released through Bristol city council.

"Said Mr Hamblin: 'I was determined to get the flat that is overlooking the waterfront. I knew there were at least 20 people interested so I got here early'.

"At 8 a.m. yesterday Cheryl Matthews and her boyfriend Wayne Collins joined the queue as did Mr Don Duon, which meant all four flats were taken.

"Said Mr Duon: 'I would think about 100 people have walked up and gone away when they realised that there was a queue of four and all the flats would go.

"'I have even been offered money for my place in the queue, but would not accept it'.

"Mr Hamblin said: 'I may not even move in. There are another eight flats being released next week and I understand that the price may rise by £2,000.

"'With that sort of money being made, I may sell the flat without moving in to the highest bidder.

"'To buy a property in the centre of Bristol overlooking the waterfront will be very difficult in the future. This is a tremendous area, which is improving all the time and is so close to the heart of the city'.

"The interest in the flats has been so high that the sales office does not open on Saturdays—it does not need to.

"The flats, which have a view of Bristol Bridge, are part of an urban renewal development by Bristol city council and Lovell Homes."

1988

SUNDAY MAY 29TH

We'd watched them go up in the 60s and 70s. And towards the end of the 80s we watched one of them come down in the most spectacular act of demolition since the Luftwaffe began blitzing Bristol in 1940.

Coming down was that familiar wall of concrete just off the city centre called the Canon's Marsh tobacco bonds.

For years they'd worn war-time camouflage long after hostilities ceased and then they were painted a no less obtrusive off-white colour which didn't do the look of central Bristol a great deal of good.

So when Lloyds at last won its bid to move its headquarters to Bristol's increasingly attractive dockside, and when Bristolians learned it would mean demolishing the tobacco bonds, everyone said: 'And about time too'.

Lloyd's went one stage further. They decided to turn the demolition into a public event and announced that it would take place at 7 a.m. on a Sunday.

No-one who was there will ever forget it. I was lucky, invited to the VIP area directly in front of the warehouses. We were served early morning bacon sandwiches and a Bucks Fizz of sparkling wine and orange juice.

Other companies with offices overlooking the site did the same. It was early morning party time and it was impossible to count the gigantic crowds who turned out to see the biggest bang. 100,000? Maybe. Perhaps even more.

It was raining at 5 a.m. Half an hour later the clouds fled. By 6.55 a.m. the air was so clear you could almost touch the Dundry hills if you were standing in the city looking south.

A tiny camera-carrying model aircraft was started up just in front of us. It wobbled, weaved and took off. Then came the bang of the warning maroon flare. And then came the blast itself. Monday's Post reported:

"At 7 a.m. yesterday Bristol had its ugly, unloved tobacco warehouses. One crunching, crumping, heart-stopping bang later and they shuddered, cracked, heaved and finally vanished in a blinding cloud of dust.

"It was a marvellous moment. Photographers cursed because their cameras had shaken, some of Bristol's leading planners shook fists in the air in sheer exultation, dignitaries stood open-mouthed in awe and the thousands and thousands who'd left home at dawn to pack every vantage point cheered and cheered and cheered.

"The moment I'll never forget came in the aftermath as a great plume of dust grew and grew and grew over Canon's Marsh and VIPs scurried for shelter from its relentless, menacing advance.

"For a minute or two I stood utterly alone as everyone hid from the blinding, choking, clothes-and-hair covering dust with its acrid taste of stale tobacco.

"It hid the sun and it hid the sky until, at last, the palest edge of blue filtered through.

"And as the dust gently drifted below the skyline first the masts of the s.s. *Great Britain* appeared and then the lunatic sight of huge, rafted heaps of white concrete where the warehouses once stood.

"It was demolition expert Mr Charles Moran's encore and he well deserved his second round of applause when that breath-taking sight came into view."

Going . . .

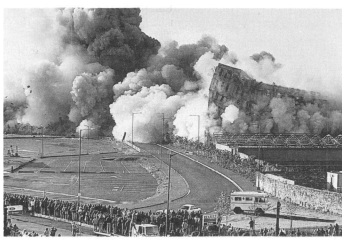

Going . . .

Gone.

EVENING POST

★★★

Thursday, February 23, 1989

RAC RESCUE SERVICES

The shattered windows on the fourth floor of the building

Police fear terror campaign after university blast

BEWARE BOMBERS

JOHN HARLAND
... blast fears

Reports: Martin Powell, Ian Onions, Ben Preston, Nigel Heath and Paul Fluck Pictures: Charles Breton

Police fear the blast that through the university's administration early today the start of the campaign.

Chief Con-stable John Harland said today: "It was a wanton act by a person, or group of people, who absolutely had no care for the safety of human life.

"It may be that this crime heralds the start of something in the form of a campaign."

He warned institutions, like the university, or fur shops, which are freely accessible to the public, to be on their guard.

Vice-chancellor Sir John Kingman said the university would con-tinue as normally as pos-sible.

"We will not let this deflect from our purpose," he said.

Forensic experts and Army bomb disposal ex-perts were examining the scene today.

The blast ripped a hole in the fourth-floor ceiling

and blew a hole in the floor. Water pipes were damaged and the heavy plate-glass windows blew out, showering glass into the car park of the nearby Hawthorns Hotel.

Flooding

Hotel worker Mr David Dowty said: "I was get-ting ready to come off duty. I heard an almighty bang and saw a big blue flash, and there was a shower of glass all over the road."

University spokesman Mr Don Carleton said the violence of the blast was such that if anyone had been walking in the vicinity they would have been killed or seriously hurt.

"There is nothing we do at the university that would merit this kind of attack," he said.

One theory being followed by the police is

"However, we equally well know these people act as judge, jury and executioner. The first you know about any charge they make is when it explodes."

Flooding caused by fractured water pipes may have damaged the university's computers.

After yesterday's warning the building was evacuated and sniffer dogs were used to search the area. It was given the all-clear at 3pm.

Mr Harland said he could not say for sure whether the bomb was planted before yester-day's search.

"Our sniffer dogs are very thorough, but it is a reality that the device could have been there when we searched," he said.

University vice-chancellor Sir John Kingman, right, points out the damage to Education Secretary Kenneth Baker

'WE MUST CONDEMN THESE FANATICS'

Education Secre-tary Mr Kenneth Baker, speaking out-side the bombed building this after-noon, said: "This is an appalling example of terrorism.

"Fanatics who reach for the bomb have to be condemned. They have no excuses. They have no justifi-cations.

"This bomb is bad news for a civilised society.

"Universities en-shrine free speech and measured arguments.

"They should not be scenes of violence and intolerance."

Mr Baker had broken off from a Cabinet meeting to visit Bristol today.

MORE REPORTS AND PICTURES, PAGE 3
POST VIEW, PAGE 6

Turn to page 3

TV GUIDE Page 25 · WEATHER Page 2 CLASSIFIED Page 28 · SERVICE SPOT Page 24 BUSINESS Pages 96 and 97 · **25 Pages of JOBS**

1989

Bristol had suffered the Luftwaffe blitzes of World War II and two bombing attacks by the IRA in the 1970s. The 1980s closed with a bizarre new brand of violent terrorism ... from the Animal Lib bomber.

"The Senate House in Tyndall Avenue, Clifton exploded in a blue flash just after midnight and Army bomb disposal experts said that a 5lb bomb was responsible.

"It was planted in the corner of a bar on the fourth floor of the building.

"The blast happened 12 hours after police bomb experts, with sniffer dogs, searched the building, following warning calls to two newspapers—one the Evening Post—by a man claiming to represent the Animal Abused Society.

"Forensic experts and Army bomb disposal experts were examining the scene today.

"The blast ripped a hole in the fourth-floor ceiling and blew a hole in the floor. Water pipes were damaged and the heavy plate-glass windows blew out, showering glass into the car park of the nearby Hawthorns Hotel.

"Hotel worker Mr David Dowty said: 'I was getting ready to come off duty. I heard an almighty bang and saw a big blue flash, and there was a shower of glass all over the road.'

"University spokesman Mr Don Carleton said the violence of the blast was such that if anyone had been walking in the vicinity they would have been killed or seriously hurt.

" 'There is nothing we do at the university that would merit this kind of attack' he said.

" 'However, we equally well know these people act as judge, jury and executioner. The first you know about any charge they make is when it explodes.'

"One theory being followed by police is that the bomb had a timing device and the bombers may have thought it would go off at noon yesterday instead of midnight.

" 'A device of the power which was involved here could have killed many, many people' said Dep. Chief Constable John Harland.

"The bar in Senate House is not used by students. Police were checking groups that may have hired rooms in the block recently.

"Bristol West MP Mr William Waldegrave said: 'There must be people in our city who know who these madmen are. I urge them to contact the police before there is loss of life.'

"Education Secretary Mr Kenneth Baker broke off from a Cabinet meeting to visit Bristol.

"Mr Baker, speaking outside the bombed building this afternoon said: 'This is an appalling act of terrorism.

" 'Fanatics who reach for the bomb have to be condemned. They have no excuses. They have no justifications.

" 'This bomb is bad news for a civilised society.

" 'Universities enshrine free speech and measured arguments. They should not be scenes of violence and intolerance.' "

1990

THURSDAY NOVEMBER 22ND

Maggie Quits, the Post's blazing front page read as news of the fall of the Premier who had become almost part of the British landscape echoed around the world.

The resignation had been rumoured the night before. When the confirmation finally came, the Post's editorial team had already prepared seven pages of news and background on the story of the year and a four-page supplement on The Thatcher Years.

Political editor Michael Lord gave his view in a special On Politics column that afternoon.

"We will miss her.

"She was argumentative, domineering, bossy, vain and not above twisting the truth like any other politician.

"But she was a leader of towering personality, guts and vision. Things will not be the same now, whoever takes over.

"The men in grey suits—whether glamorous like Heseltine or studious like Hurd—are back.

"Mrs Thatcher arrived at 10 Downing Street preaching the words of St Francis of Assisi, promising harmony, truth, faith and hope.

"By her own standards, she succeeded in at least three of those. But harmony always eluded her.

"She changed the direction of Britain in a way no Prime Minister has ever done before. She taught us all—workers, unions, bosses, ancient institutions—that there is no such thing as a free lunch.

"She may have known the cost of everything and the value of nothing, but the lessons she taught have turned Britain round.

"Intellectuals, literary and media folk scorned her as that suburban grocer's daughter with a net-curtain mind. But in three general elections, the public disagreed.

"With their backing in votes, she took on—and took out—the unions, sold off every conceivable public utility, slaughtered sacred cows by the herd and blasted her way through the bedrock of British institutions in a way unthinkable in any other politician.

"She leaves Britain a nation of car phones and cardboard cities, of vulgar wealth and broken sewers.

"She leaves Britain an uncontestably richer nation than she found it. But she also leaves it harsher, uglier, more confident and basically more divided.

"Whatever her mistakes, her chillingly warlike attitude to any problem, domestic or international, her obstinacy, her economies with truth, she has stamped her mark on the nation and the world.

"It was Thatcher who first spotted Gorbachev's stature. It is Thatcher the rest of the world—and especially Eastern Europe—sees as the friend of freedom and enterprise.

"But in Britain, Thatcher is a name as often spat out as praised.

"Yet, typically, she has stunned us all by taking the advice that must have caused her more anguish than any other in 15 years of leadership: the advice to go.

"She always said she would not hang on, that she would know when the time came to quit.

"Everyone else doubted. Right up to this morning they doubted.

"That was her very last surprise. At the end, she did not break the unwritten rules, she obeyed them.

"Yes, we will miss her."

1991

THURSDAY JANUARY 17TH

The day marked the start of a new technological war reported by a new tech media across the world.

Within minutes of the launch of the air assault on Saddam Hussein's Iraq, the Post was up and running with preparations for an eight-page supplement on the war, its background, the local units who'd be fighting, the Middle East situation and detailed accounts of the airborne hardware being flung at Iraqi targets.

Reporters and specialist writers hurried out a comprehensive account of the news so far and the background to the news.

Experts were interviewed, memories gathered from veterans of the not-so-long ago Falklands war and the strategic strength of the allies which had formed into the American-led force was analysed and explained. And all this was on the streets of Bristol within a handful of hours of the start of the blitz on Saddam.

Information flowed into the Post's building on Temple Way through international news agencies feeding the computer system, through satellite and cable, through TV and radio.

And if the Post was no longer the most up-to-the-minute bringer of news to Bristol that it had been on Day One on April 18th, 1932 when the crowds flocked to Silver Street—the global village created by TV and satellite had seen to that—it played to the paper's strengths perfectly that day.

The Post offered maps to pore over, statistics to study, detailed information to check and re-check as the days went by and a detailed analysis of how the two sides stood at the start of an awesome moment of history.

The Post asked General Sir Jeremy Moore, the retired commander of the Falklands campaign who had settled in the West Country, for his view of how the British contingent would react when the bombing stopped—and the land battle inevitably began.

" 'Troops know if someone is wounded in battle, the medics will deal with him and so they get on with their job. But after the battle there is a quiet, a kind of shock.

" 'It is then you notice the appalling filth, bodies, excreta and discarded equipment. It puts a tremendous stress on people.'

"But the General went on: 'I always think that it is worse for the families. The strain on them is far greater in some ways.

" 'Soldiers spend their lives preparing for battle. There are risks but that is part of a soldier's life. It is very different for his family back home. They just have to sit and wait.

" 'They must keep writing to the troops, that is absolutely vital. I remember in the Falklands getting a letter from my wife immediately before the final battle.

" 'It was a marvellous boost. I knew then we were going to win. But it really made me feel terrific.

" 'It is vital that our troops know they have the support of the people back home.

" 'Families should also communicate with each other. Get together so they can talk and support each other.' "

These were prophetic words. The swift battles that followed did reveal all the horrors he had spoken of . . . and the families of the units from Yeovilton and other bases formed self-help groups that were second to none.

And it was all reported in the *Evening Post*.

103